Elements of Indigenous Style

Elements of Indigenous Style

A GUIDE FOR WRITING BY AND ABOUT INDIGENOUS PEOPLES

Gregory Younging

www.brusheducation.ca

23 24 25 10 9 8

Printed and manufactured in Canada

Brush Education Inc.
www.brusheducation.ca
contact@brusheducation.ca

Cover image: istock: OGphoto

Cover and interior design: Carol Dragich, Dragich Design
Proofreading: Shauna Babiuk
Index: Stephen Ullstrom

Contributors
Mary Cardinal Collins
Warren Cariou
Sophie McCall

Library and Archives Canada Cataloguing in Publication
Younging, Gregory, author
    Elements of Indigenous style : a guide for writing by and about Indigenous Peoples / Gregory Younging.

Includes bibliographical references and index.
Issued in print and electronic formats.

ISBN 978-1-55059-716-5 (softcover).--ISBN 978-1-55059-717-2 (PDF).--
ISBN 978-1-55059-718-9 (Kindle).--ISBN 978-1-55059-719-6 (EPUB)

    1. Authorship--Style manuals. 2. Authorship--Handbooks, manuals, etc.
3. Native authors--Canada. 4. Native peoples in literature. 5. Ethnography--
Authorship--Style manuals. I. Title.

PN147.Y68 2018   808.02   C2017-908038-5   C2017-908039-3

We acknowledge the support of the Government of Canada
Nous reconnaissons l'appui du gouvernement du Canada | Canadä

Indigenous peoples have the right to maintain, control, protect and develop their cultural heritage, traditional knowledge and traditional cultural expressions, as well as the manifestations of their sciences, technologies and cultures, including human and genetic resources, seeds, medicines, knowledge of the properties of fauna and flora, oral traditions, literatures, designs, sports and traditional games and visual and performing arts. They also have the right to maintain, control, protect and develop their intellectual property over such cultural heritage, traditional knowledge, and traditional cultural expressions.

—Article 31, United Nations Declaration on the
Rights of Indigenous Peoples, 2007

Contents

Foreword

This book is an extremely important, timely, and well-thought-out resource. It is an excellent guide for publishers, academics, journalists, students, and anyone else who is interested in writing about Indigenous Peoples. Greg Younging's extraordinary experience, cultural sensitivity, and knowledge base come through on every page, providing readers with very thoughtful and helpful advice on so many areas of potential difficulty. I can see that this book will have very wide relevance even beyond Canada's borders, though it is well focused on the Canadian context.

The book is written in an eloquent, intimate style that puts readers at ease and positions them as participants in a conversation—a technique that works exceedingly well for the chosen purpose. There is a great need for a resource of this kind, and *Elements of Indigenous Style* fits that need in a resoundingly positive and productive way. Over time, I feel that this book will make a significant difference in the fair and equitable representation of Indigenous Peoples, and this will lead to empowerment and pride among Indigenous community members.

In addition to the invaluable advice contained in the book's editorial principles, the word-usage examples are extremely helpful. The discussion of rights, intellectual property, and the public domain is excellent, as is the material on Métis identity and community history. Throughout the book, the discussion of problematic practices is done in a clear and thoughtful way, explaining *why* a particular practice is disrespectful or inaccurate. Thus, it comes across not as a prescriptive and authoritarian book (as some writing textbooks do), but rather as a teaching text that informs readers of why certain editorial practices are problematic, and how these situations can be avoided. This book provides solutions rather than solely identifying problems.

Possibly the most important ethos of this book is contained in the advice that there is no substitute for engaging in a relationship with the Indigenous Peoples who are represented in a text. This book foregrounds the Indigenous methodology of working from the basis of relationships, and thus it is an excellent example of decolonial scholarship.

Warren Cariou
Canada Research Chair in Narrative, Community, and Indigenous Cultures
Director, Centre for Creative Writing and Oral Culture
Professor, Department of English, Film, and Theatre
University of Manitoba

Preface

This book represents the first published editorial principles and guidelines for works written by or about Indigenous Peoples. I am not putting these principles and guidelines forward as quintessential. This book is, indeed, a first attempt at an Indigenous style guide and a first volume. I fully intend that Indigenous and non-Indigenous publishers and editors, and other interested parties, will consider these as *proposed* principles and guidelines, and provide feedback that will inform subsequent editions.

Some elements of a higher level of authenticity in Indigenous works are currently in a state of evolution and flux, such that a comprehensive style guide is not yet possible. Here's an example: we are in an era when Indigenous Nations are rejecting the colonial names that have been applied to and imposed on them, and are reclaiming their original names. Inuit were among the first to reject the term *Eskimo* in the 1970s; since then, many Indigenous Peoples have been bringing the word their ancestors called themselves back into use.

This phenomenon is occurring across the continent, hemisphere, and world, but not with any degree of consistency. In addition, in some cases, a range of spellings exists for some of these original names.

Consequently, with this and some other issues in the following chapters, I have attempted to state best current practices and I hope that more comprehensive solutions will be developed in future editions of this book or in future work by others. I am also fully open to critique on the propositions I am making in this book and to considering other arguments and opinions, which I'm sure will lead to improvements in subsequent volumes. As this book is published,

The Chicago Manual of Style is in its seventeenth edition, and I hope there will be many editions of this Indigenous style guide as well.

I am not the sole authority, but merely someone who has been working on these issues and has been encouraged to put the first Indigenous style guide out there for consideration. Still, I am confident that this guide will be useful to editors and publishers, and that it has the potential to lead to better works by and about Indigenous Peoples. I hope you will at least find it as interesting and thought provoking as I have.

I would like to thank the contributors: Mary Cardinal Collins, Dr. Warren Cariou, Marc Côté, Lee Maracle, Dr. Sophie McCall, Dr. Deanna Reder, Glenn Rollans, Bruce Walsh, and Wendy Whitebear. I would also like to thank the peer reviewers Dr. Warren Cariou and Dr. Sophie McCall, and Lauri Seidlitz and Lynn Zwicky for their editorial assistance.

Gregory Younging

Introduction

In 1989, I had some of my poetry included in an anthology by the Indigenous publishing house Theytus Books called *Seventh Generation*. I was thrilled to be published for the first time.

In 1990, some of my work was published again by Theytus Books. I was an aspiring writer fresh out of university and the book was the first volume of *Gatherings: The En'owkin Journal of First North American Peoples*. At that time, there was an excitement running through Indigenous communities about the first journal in North America that would publish a current sampling of Indigenous Literatures each year.

The following year, I was asked to be managing editor of Theytus Books. Although I was young and inexperienced, I could not turn down the challenge of working with the first Indigenous owned and operated press in Canada (which had been founded in 1980), and so I found myself editor of *Gatherings* Volume II in 1991 and Volume III in 1992.

Over the years—as I worked on fifteen volumes of *Gatherings*, and published or edited more than four hundred Indigenous authors and one hundred Theytus titles—I found myself perplexed by a number of editorial problems pertaining specifically to the publishing of material by or about Indigenous Peoples. Gradually, as more and more unique problems came up in the course of editing, it became apparent that Theytus Books, as an Indigenous publisher, needed to establish editorial guidelines on several specific matters to set standards and ensure consistency.

Working at Theytus has provided many opportunities to discuss these editorial issues with Indigenous writers, editors, and publishers, many of whom have offered their ideas, opinions, and proposed solutions. There have also been valuable discussions with non-Indigenous fiction and nonfiction writers, academics, journalists, and editors. Many of those people also indicated that editorial guidelines would be of great use to them in their work. Based on those discussions, it became apparent that a set of specific editorial guidelines adhering to Indigenous cultural, political, and literary concerns was not only necessary for Theytus, but would also have wider application.

The first draft of this style guide was my Master's project in 1999. In many ways, my thinking about Indigenous editing and publishing has not changed since then. This is partly because Indigenous Peoples have enduring positions on many issues, and the ways to approach and respect Indigenous Peoples are also enduring. It's also partly because colonialism remains a troubled context for editing and publishing in Canada (and everything else). We need a new relationship between Indigenous Peoples and settler people. That has been true my whole working life, and remains true.

In the last five to ten years, though, I've seen major improvement in editing and publishing Indigenous authors and Indigenous content, even by non-Indigenous editors and publishers. There's a growing awareness that you can't just "take the stories." In the 1990s, during intense discourses on cultural appropriation, I used to say that non-Indigenous people should just stop writing about Indigenous Peoples. Now that I've seen good collaborations and respectful work, I don't say that anymore.

Indigenous Peoples seek to collaborate with publishers to make the publishing industry—this important industry—more inclusive. Indigenous authors, editors, and publishers work to create titles that reflect the highest levels of understanding, and authentic meaningful stories, and truth telling. So, too, should all authors, editors, and publishers. I hope *Elements of Indigenous Style* is useful in this endeavour.

1

Why an Indigenous style guide?

The need to Indigenize publishing

The paramount purpose of literature focusing on a specific cultural group should be to present the culture in a realistic and insightful manner, with the highest possible degree of verisimilitude. However, the body of literature on Indigenous Peoples mostly fails to achieve this standard. The failure has been a long-standing concern of Indigenous Peoples in Canada.

The failure comes from a colonial practice of transmitting "information" about Indigenous Peoples rather than transmitting Indigenous Peoples' perspectives about themselves. The anthropologist Franz Boas put a name on this perspective in the mid-twentieth century. He called it *ethnocentrism*, which he recognized as a barrier to cultural understanding. Cultural understanding, he realized, can only be achieved by a "perspective from the inside." Indigenous and other scholars have since coined other terms for this perspective, such as *Eurocentrism*, and have written about, for example, the *British-centrism* of Canada.

Some members of the Canadian literary establishment have also long recognized the damage of this perspective. Margaret Atwood wrote in 1972, "The Indians and Eskimos have rarely been considered in and for themselves: they are usually made into projections of something in the white Canadian psyche."[1]

The need to Indigenize writing, editing, and publishing in many ways parallels the evolution of writing about African Americans and women in the late twentieth century, and the development of concepts such as "Black History" and "Herstory." Indigenous writers, editors, and publishers have asserted that the experience of being an Indigenous person is profoundly different from that of other people in North America. Many Indigenous Peoples and authors have cited cultural appropriation, misrepresentation, and lack of respect for Indigenous cultural Protocols as significant problems in Canadian publishing. Indigenous Peoples have frequently taken the stand that they are best capable of, and morally empowered to, transmit information about themselves. They have the right to tell their own story. When an author is writing about them—even in established genres such as anthropological studies, history, and political commentary— Indigenous Peoples would at least like the opportunity for input into how they are represented on the page.

Indigenous Peoples add their voices to the argument that it is important for *any* national or cultural group to have input into the documentation of its history, philosophies, and reality as a basic matter of cultural integrity. In some respects, this is *especially* pressing for Indigenous Peoples in Canada and other parts of the world, because they have been misrepresented for so long, which has created a body of literature inconsistent with, and often opposed to, Indigenous cultural understandings.

In *So You Want to Write About American Indians*, Devon Abbott Mihesuah writes, "If you plan on writing about Natives you must know much more about them, such as tribal history, their language, religion, gender roles, appearances, politics, creation stories, how they dealt with Europeans, and how they have survived to the present day."[2] Mihesuah further contends, "Can you secure tribal permission for your topic? If you are doing a serious study of a tribe, you can not do the work adequately without conversing with knowledgeable members of the tribes."[3]

Some improvements in Canadian publishing have come from a slow awakening to the impact of colonial ethnocentrism on who has been writing about Indigenous Peoples, with what process, and in what words. But works are still being produced that contain old stereotypes and perceptions, and that lack respect for Indigenous Protocols and perspectives. In 2017, for example, I asked a well-respected Indigenous colleague, who works as a freelance editor and validator of Indigenous content in a variety of Canadian publishing contexts, for examples of projects that had gone well from her point of view. Her frustration showed in her answer, which was "really none."

Many Canadian publishers have a sense that they're not editing work by and about Indigenous Peoples as well as they could. For the most part, they want to do it right, but often they don't know how to do it right. Part of the solution is to develop and train more Indigenous editors and publishers, so they can work in publishing. Part of the solution is also to train more non-Indigenous editors and publishers so they can better work on Indigenous titles. I take heart from the responses of the more than forty Indigenous and Canadian editors who attended the Indigenous Editors Circle (IEC) and Editing Indigenous Manuscripts (EIM) courses offered at Humber College in Toronto in August 2017.[4] The IEC faculty (which I was part of until 2017) has been surprised by the increased number of Canadian publishers who are interested in attending the sessions.

Another part of the solution is to recognize work already in progress. Indigenous writers, editors, and publishers are developing and defining emerging contemporary Indigenous Literatures, and they are establishing culturally based Indigenous methodologies within the editing and publishing process.

This style guide aims also to be part of the solution—part of the process of instilling Indigenous Peoples in the heart of Canadian publishing.

Case study: University of Regina Press

University of Regina Press is an example, among several examples, of a Canadian publishing house with a deliberate mix of Indigenous and non-Indigenous staff. This case study presents perspectives from within the press on this choice.

WENDY WHITEBEAR, OFFICE MANAGER AND MANUSCRIPT REVIEWER

Wendy Whitebear is Cree-Saulteaux* from White Bear First Nation.

Honouring Indigenous ways of knowing, our stories, needs to be meaningful—more than a box checked off in a list of things to do for reconciliation. We know these stories: they are our stories, we have lived them. Mainstream society does not yet know them and does not yet value them.

Around the table at the press, I find the significance of Indigenous content can get missed. When Indigenous people talk to each other, we have our own ways of thinking and knowing. We understand each other. *I* can *hear* what an Indigenous person is really saying, what they actually mean. Non-Indigenous people don't have that context. They need help to see through our lens. So, I'm often telling stories from my own family, and from my own experience as an Indigenous woman and activist working for the betterment of her own people.

The Education of Augie Merasty** is about context, too. It doesn't just talk about residential schools. It speaks to the human experience of it. You feel empathy as an Indigenous person, as the story is ours. Others have no real understanding. To them, abuse is just a word and they comment on our true history by saying "oh it was bad." The book speaks to the fact that the experience was horrific for the ones who had to live it. The reader has a deeper understanding and can experience real empathy.

I have strong convictions about the Indigenous perspective being told. I have a problem when a book comes out "*about* us, but not *with* us"—when no one has consulted the family of the story or an

---

* This spelling follows the preference of Wendy Whitebear.

** *The Education of Augie Merasty: A Residential School Memoir*, by Joseph Auguste Merasty, with David Carpenter, was published by University of Regina Press in 2015.

Elder to ensure Protocols are being followed. So I check for that, and ask questions about that. Our team is diligent about ensuring that the authors are taking these steps—however, not all publishers are. Our history and our stories are continually being told from a colonial perspective and therefore lack the magnitude of the atrocities that happened and the resilience of our people.

I want to Indigenize the publishing industry. Indigenous ways of knowing and being should inform the work of publishing. I would like to see a future where this is usual and ordinary, like the pen on your desk.

BRUCE WALSH, PUBLISHER

University of Regina Press currently has three Indigenous staff: a student, an intern, and our business manager. Every week, we have a staff meeting where everything is discussed, from timelines to manuscript development to marketing. Each book is pulled apart in terms of content and everyone weighs in on positioning, packaging, and how the books speak to our brand.

Having Indigenous perspectives around the table has changed the press. From the beginning (the press launched in 2013) we have taken great care with Indigenous content by consulting Elders and getting community approval when appropriate. But discussions were almost theoretical then. Now, with the input of Cree, Saulteaux, and Métis staff, we are much more grounded in community—things have come into sharper focus. They hear subtle bias in wording. They suggest approaches for finding information and who to talk to. It's a very, very rich conversation.

In one meeting, we discussed a project about RCMP-Indigenous relations, in which staff shared stories of how their parents and grandparents hid in the woods to avoid residential school. Conversations about Indigenous trauma—or Indigenous joy—are real. We've shed tears around that table, but we also do a lot of laughing. With dozens and dozens of Nations in Canada, no one individual can speak for all Indigenous Peoples. So having more than one perspective is important. It helps make the office a safe space and encourages conversation.

Every year, the press hires a new Indigenous intern. We think of it as developing capacity from the ground up. We hope that the apprenticeship process—how we really learn publishing—means that one day our interns will be running the press.

Principles of Indigenous style

The twenty-two principles of this style guide are placed in the context of the discussion where they arise.

They are also collected at the end of the guide as an appendix.

Here is the first principle, based on the discussion on the previous page about the need to Indigenize publishing:

PRINCIPLE 1: THE PURPOSE OF INDIGENOUS STYLE

The purpose of Indigenous style is to produce works that:

- reflect Indigenous realities as they are perceived by Indigenous Peoples
- are truthful and insightful in their Indigenous content
- are respectful of the cultural integrity of Indigenous Peoples

---

The place of non-Indigenous style guides

This style guide does not replace standard references on editing and publishing, such as *The Chicago Manual of Style* or the *MLA Handbook*. Neither does it replace the house styles of individual publishers.

You should still follow these styles, in general, when you are writing, editing, or publishing Indigenous authors and Indigenous content. In some cases, however, Indigenous style and conventional style or house style will not agree. When that happens, Indigenous style should override conventional style and house style. If you are not familiar with Indigenous style, this may not feel right to you at first. Indigenous style uses more capitalization than conventional style, for example, and it incorporates Indigenous Protocols, which require time and attention to observe correctly.

It is helpful to keep in mind that Indigenous style is part of a conversation that aims to build a new relationship between Indigenous people and settler society. Indigenous style is conversing with you, perhaps for the first time, in an ongoing decolonizing discourse.

PRINCIPLE 2: WHEN INDIGENOUS STYLE AND CONVENTIONAL STYLES DISAGREE

Works by Indigenous authors or with Indigenous content should follow standard style references and house styles, except where these disagree with Indigenous style.

In these works, Indigenous style overrules other styles in cases of disagreement.

2

A history of the portrayal of Indigenous Peoples in literature

The foundation of settler society's perception of Indigenous Peoples

Early writings about Indigenous Peoples were authored by explorers such as Samuel de Champlain and Jacques Cartier in the 1500s and 1600s, missionaries such as John McDougall in the 1800s, anthropologists such as Diamond Jenness and Franz Boas around the turn of the century, and literary writers such as James Fenimore Cooper and Stephen Leacock in the early-to-mid 1900s. Most of these writers referred to Indigenous Peoples as an inferior, vanishing race— a description that is degrading and offensive to most Indigenous Peoples for obvious reasons, and inaccurate in ways that still escape some Canadian publishers and editors today.

In *The Indians of Canada* (1932), which was for decades considered *the* authoritative anthropological text, Diamond Jenness writes in the first paragraph: "When Samuel Champlain in 1603 sailed up the St. Lawrence river and agreed to support the Algonkian Indians at Tadoussac against the aggression of the Iroquois, he could not foresee that the petty strife between those two apparently insignificant hordes of 'savages' would one day decide the fate of New France."[5]

Most of the literature written by explorers, missionaries, and anthropologists provided little insight into the cultural realities of Indigenous Peoples. Yet, this literature influenced the intellectual foundations of settler society, in its perception of Indigenous Peoples as primitive and underdeveloped. Indigenous intellectuals, such as the late John Mohawk, have further argued that Darwinian concepts—construed, consciously or subconsciously, to locate Indigenous Peoples somewhere on the evolutionary scale between primates and *Homo sapiens*—also shaped settler society perception.

It was a perception conveyed in the work of high-profile Canadian literary writers, such as Farley Mowat and Stephen Leacock, whose mainstream popularity served to reinforce it.

Imposter literature

Imposters such as Grey Owl and Chief Buffalo Child Long Lance had considerable notoriety lecturing, writing, and publishing while masquerading as Indigenous people (although Long Lance did have some Indigenous ancestry). Generally, these writers displayed a less condescending and more positive attitude toward Indigenous Peoples, although their work tended to reinforce the stereotypical image of Indigenous Peoples as glorified remnants of the past, *à la* notions of the noble savage. As noted by Robert Berkhofer in *The White Man's Indian: Images of the American Indian from Columbus to the Present*, "Although each succeeding generation presumed its imagery based more upon the Native American of observation and report, the Indian of imagination and ideology continued to be derived as much from the polemical and creative needs of Whites as from what they heard and read of actual Native Americans or even at times experienced."[6]

The legacy of the charlatan tradition set by Grey Owl and Long Lance was evident in the work of writers such as Jamake Highwater and Lynn Andrews in the 1980s. It may have also played a role in the 2017 controversy about Canadian author Joseph Boyden, which led to a highly public discourse on issues of Indigenous identity and authenticity.

Non-Indigenous academic writing

From the 1980s to the present, a wave of writing by non-Indigenous academics has taken place. Many of these authors are involved with higher-level academic and government institutions, and have established themselves as authoritative Indigenous experts. The majority of these writers are knowledgeable and supportive of Indigenous Peoples' political and cultural aspirations, and they must also be credited with increased public awareness of these aspirations in recent years. Writers such as Michael Asch, Thomas Berger, Menno Boldt, Ken Coates, Jaskiran Dhillon, Allison Hargreaves, J. R. Miller, Bradford Morse, Rick Ponting, John Ralston Saul, Sally Weaver, and others, are part of this tradition, which has evolved into an important category that could be referred to as "allied academic literature."

However, while much of this body of work has observational and analytical value, it has ultimately not expressed Indigeneity and Indigenous epistemologies, nor has it expressed Indigenous Peoples' internal unique perspectives on contemporary Indigenous political and cultural issues. Although this body of work is predominately well intentioned, some Indigenous writers, such as Lee Maracle, Leroy Little Bear, and the late Howard Adams, have stated that it can tend to reduce emotionally, historically, and culturally charged issues to dry information laden with legalized or academic jargon. As stated by Adams, "Academia is slow to reexamine what has been accepted for centuries. . . . These myths have been so deeply ingrained in the peoples' psyche that even Aboriginals will have to go to great lengths to rid themselves of colonial ideologies."[7] It should be noted, however, that the Indigenous allied academic movement has progressed and evolved to the point that this could change and, perhaps, is beginning to change.

A view commonly held by many Indigenous Peoples—as well as many mainstream historians and academics—is that contemporary literature conveys an improved portrayal of Indigenous Peoples, but that some of it also persists in conveying subtle inappropriate stereotypes and faulty academic paradigms.

The Indigenous Voice

The creation and expression of culture by Indigenous Peoples—through any traditional medium, or any contemporary medium, or any combination of these—constitutes what can be referred to as the "Indigenous Voice."

The contemporary Indigenous Voice is a unique mode of cultural expression that draws from a blend of traditional and contemporary sources such as Oral Traditions; techniques of Traditional Storytelling; film; inanimate, animal, and spirit characters from Traditional Stories; Indigenous historical perspectives; and contemporary Indigenous existence.

Beginning in the 1980s, Indigenous authors have developed and expressed the Indigenous Voice in works that now form distinct, culturally based, contemporary literary forms. These works are the most culturally authentic literary expression of Indigenous realities. Canadian literary organizations and publishers are beginning to realize the significance of these literary forms, after years of marginalizing Indigenous authors through lack of understanding and access. To date, works by Indigenous authors are overshadowed by a greater number of books about Indigenous Peoples written by non-Indigenous authors, who continue to develop a separate body of literature about Indigenous Peoples.

The Indigenous Voice, Traditional Knowledge, and Oral Traditions

The Indigenous Voice is in dialogue with Oral Traditions and Traditional Knowledge—a process alive with connection and transformation. The Indigenous Voice speaks from the continuum of Traditional Stories that have been told on Indigenous Territories for millennia as part of Oral Traditions. These stories are spiritually connected to the land, ancestors, and the particular Indigenous Nation they come from.

A few definitions might be helpful here. Oral Traditions comprise the stories that have been told for generations, many of which are Sacred Stories. Traditional Knowledge is a wider category: it includes, for example, Indigenous architecture; forest management with fire; medicines and herbology; and knowledge about climate patterns and animal migrations. Traditional Knowledge also includes Oral Traditions. For the most part, Traditional Knowledge is not sacred—but some of it is. The United Nations World Intellectual Property Organization (WIPO) refers to Traditional Knowledge that is sacred as "secret and sacred." Traditional Knowledge contains Sacred Stories within Oral Traditions and sacred aspects of, for example, medicines and herbology. Mostly, though, Traditional Knowledge is information.[8]

Extreme caution should be practised in editing and publishing Traditional Knowledge, especially in editing and publishing Indigenous Oral Traditions. Indigenous collaboration and consultation are essential. Publishers should be prepared to find out that, in some cases, publishing Traditional Knowledge is not appropriate. In addition, they should seek the skills of Indigenous editors, and they should assign authorship and copyright properly. Authorship and copyright rest with the Indigenous People who are the source of the Traditional Knowledge.

The many vast pools of information held by individual Indigenous Nations have been transmitted orally over centuries, and comprise unique bodies of knowledge with distinct cultural content. This oral transmission has often worked in conjunction with physical methods of documentation, such as dramatic productions, dance performances, petroglyphs, scrolls, Totem Poles, Wampum Belts, and masks.

Traditional Knowledge and Oral Traditions fit the definition of publishing—which is, as my professor of publishing at Simon Fraser University, Ralph Hancox, stated it, "the transference of intellectual property from one mind to another mind, or from one mind to many other minds." If you render them in the language of European concepts, as much as it is possible, it could be said that Traditional Knowledge and Oral Traditions are traditional Indigenous publishing, and the contemporary Indigenous Voice is Indigenous Literature.

It *could* be said this way, but it's important to note how awkward it is in the context of Indigenous Peoples, who are diverse and distinct.

Contemporary Indigenous Literatures

Indigenous *Peoples* have Indigenous *Literatures*. The singular form ("Indigenous Literature") is pan-Indigenous—an umbrella term like *European literature* (which contains, for example, French literature, Irish literature, and German literature). The singular form has a place in this discussion, as a way to acknowledge Indigenous works as distinct within world (or Canadian) literature. But the singular form needs careful, informed use. It risks reinforcing an error common to colonial thinking: that what is Indigenous is all the same. In fact, Indigenous cultures in North America are far more distinct and diverse than European cultures, or Canadian and American cultures.

The Indigenous Voice contains highly meaningful and symbolic "worlds" populated with fantastic, inanimate, animal, human, and spirit characters who act out some of the most fascinating tales in world literature today. The body of natural scientific knowledge encompassed in the Indigenous Voice also contains valuable paradigms, teachings, and information that can benefit all of the world's family of nations. As sectors of the scientific and academic establishment have come to realize, Traditional Knowledge is integral to human survival.

Over the past five decades, Indigenous authors have expressed and developed the Indigenous Voice, establishing contemporary Indigenous Literatures as a new literary form.

Anishinaabe[*] author Kim Blaeser has pointed out several characteristics of contemporary Indigenous Literatures:

---

[*] This follows a spelling used by Kim Blaeser.

- They give authority to the voices of all people involved in the story, instead of a monologic voice speaking out as if it had ultimate authority.
- They give authority to the voices of animals and messages given by spirits and natural phenomena.
- They stretch across large expanses of time, ranging from ancient times to the present to the future, displaying the Indigenous concept that all time is closely connected and that actions can transcend time.[9]

Jeannette Armstrong connected to Indigenous thought in her well-known first novel *Slash* (which, in 1985, was also the first novel from a First Nations woman published in Canada). She wrote *Slash* from a first-person male perspective. Some thought this ironic, others controversial. Armstrong explained that her choice was based, in part, on Indigenous cultural beliefs that each gender is capable of assuming the characteristics of the other.[10]

Indigenous philosophy and traditions are evident in Lee Maracle's novel *Sundogs* (1992), whose style Maracle has called "Contemporary Aboriginal Voice." It is written cover to cover with no chapter breaks, and often jumps out of its own storyline to go out on a tangent, the relevance of which does not necessarily become immediately apparent. This is similar to the oratory style of an Elder speaking in a storytelling or ceremonial setting.

Tomson Highway engages Indigenous ideas about the interplay of the metaphysical and the real in his plays *The Rez Sisters* (1988); *The Sage, the Dancer and the Fool* (1989); and *Dry Lips Oughta Move to Kapuskasing* (1989); and in his first novel, *Kiss of the Fur Queen* (1998). Highway's work—with its world-rocking transitions between reality and beyond-reality, and characters that transcend these realms—imparts an ancient way of thinking and makes an important contribution to world drama and literature.

These are some of the first examples of well-known authors writing in the Indigenous Voice, and ignoring and departing from conventional European writing styles and genres. The 1980s was the second decade of Indigenous writing in Canada. Since then, these and other Indigenous authors and artists have further developed Indigenous Literatures as distinct forms.

In Canadian publishing, however, Indigenous Literatures have faced several impeding factors, for example: cultural and language barriers; the residential school system; ethnocentrism in academia; competition from non-Indigenous authors; and a lack of Indigenous-controlled editing and publishing.

Canadian publishing has also had a tendency to pigeonhole the Indigenous Voice—this important, distinct canon of literatures—as a subsection of CanLit. It is not. It comes from different traditions that developed and evolved in Indigenous Nations long before CanLit existed.

PRINCIPLE 3: INDIGENOUS LITERATURES AND CANLIT

Indigenous Literatures are their own canon and not a subgroup of CanLit. Contemporary Indigenous authors' works are an extension of Traditional Knowledge systems, Indigenous histories, histories of colonization, and contemporary realities. Indigenous Literatures frame these experiences for Indigenous readers and provide non-Indigenous readers with context for these realities.

Contemporary Indigenous Literatures connect to and extend Traditional Stories and Oral Traditions that have existed for centuries and millennia, and that long predate CanLit.

The Indigenous Voice and the individual Indigenous author

Indigenous Literatures are among the artistic disciplines where Indigenous artists are combining Traditional Knowledge (and traditional art forms) with contemporary materials, stories, and art forms.

As with other artistic disciplines, the knowledge and traditions Indigenous authors use come from their own experiences and identities—they achieve that irreplaceable "perspective from the inside" because they work from within their cultures.

Their work speaks with the most authority when their writing focuses on the Indigenous Nation they are from, and adheres to their Indigenous Protocols.

This is not to say that Indigenous authors should not write about contemporary pan-Indigenous experiences, but rather that Indigenous authors (like all authors who write about any Indigenous Nation from outside its knowledge, traditions, and realities) should consult and exercise caution when writing about Indigenous Nations other than their own.

In creating with the Indigenous Voice, Indigenous authors are using a unique form of artistic license, which is Nation-based—that is, Indigenous Nation-based. It could be termed "Indigenous National Artistic License." This gives Indigenous authors permission to innovate Traditional Knowledge, and it characterizes part of the relationship between the Indigenous artist and the Indigenous Nation to which they belong. The concept of Indigenous National Artistic License connects to the continuity, adaptability, and evolutionary nature of Indigenous ways of being in the world.

Non-Indigenous authors do not have the same artistic license. They need to enter into a relationship with the Indigenous Nation that is the source of the Traditional Knowledge and Oral Tradition they seek to use. The permission for use must come from the Nation, and must be negotiated to achieve mutually agreed terms.

3

Contemporary Indigenous cultural realities

Many common errors in editing and publishing works by Indigenous authors or with Indigenous content come from not working in a culturally appropriate way.

Working in an appropriate way begins with a clear understanding of how Indigenous Peoples perceive and contextualize their contemporary cultural realities.

Resilience and adaptation

Indigenous Peoples have undergone five hundred years of colonization by settler society, which has included attempted physical and cultural genocide, technological revolution, and the imposition of non-Indigenous legislation and institutions. Indigenous Peoples have dealt with these difficult circumstances, surviving with the foundations of their unique cultures intact.

In many cases, during the contact period, when repressive legislation and institutions were imposed on Indigenous Peoples, Indigenous institutions went underground, giving the outward appearance that they had been undermined. The reemergence of forms of traditional governments and spiritual institutions, such as the Potlatch, the Sundance, and the Longhouse, are testimony to this phenomenon.

In other cases, Indigenous Peoples made decisions to incorporate traditional institutions and aspects of culture into the contemporary context. This process of deliberate incorporation and adaptation guided Indigenous Peoples through century after century of national and cultural development before European contact. It then continued to guide them after contact—although the process was rigorously tested by the arrival of Europeans.

Indigenous Peoples have adhered to two important cultural principles in creating their unique and distinct contemporary forms:

1. Incorporating new ways of doing things should be carefully considered in consultation with Elders, traditional people, and community.

2. If it is determined that a new technology or institution goes against fundamental cultural values or might lead to negative cultural impacts, then it should not be adopted.

These principles exist, in one variation or another, in most Indigenous societies dating back to ancient times.

In applying these principles, Indigenous Peoples have responsibilities connected to internal cultural imperatives, which include telling the truth, honesty with one another, mindfulness of impacts on the community, and mindfulness of continuity with history and heritage. The ultimate responsibility for Indigenous Peoples lies in being the link between the ancestors and future generations—a cultural precept that has been referred to by Indigenous writers, such as LeAnne Howe, as "the time-space continuum."

The continuum of present, past, and future

A common mainstream perspective puts Indigenous cultures at odds with the modern world. Much writing about Indigenous Peoples by non-Indigenous authors reflects the idea that Indigenous culture is static and must exist in some past state to be authentic.

In some cases, non-Indigenous writing has implied that Indigenous cultures no longer exist at all—that mainstream settler culture has swept them away. Indigenous Peoples themselves, of course—living testaments to their presence in the present—find this perplexing.

Indigenous Peoples wish their cultures to be perceived as dynamic, in interaction with the modern world, and existing in a continuum between past and future generations of Indigenous Peoples. They are not encapsulated in the past—static and resistant to change, or absent.

Indigenous Peoples have always been adept at fitting new technologies to their cultures. Northern Cree[11] hunters, for example, have found that pursuing moose by snowmobile can add significantly to the success of hunting outings. At the same time, they still practise ancient ceremonies, such as honouring an animal's spirit in the bush upon killing, praying to and thanking the Creator, hanging the animal's bones over the doorway, and bringing the animal through the doorway backwards so the animal's spirit can leave frontwards.

Cree hunting by snowmobile is an example of what Lewis Mumford observed in the relationship between culture and technology. Mumford was a British sociologist, historian, and philosopher who thought and wrote about this relationship. He asserted that technology does not drive cultural change but, instead, responds to cultural contexts. Culture, in other words, shapes tools. With the snowmobile, the Cree continue to practise ancient ceremonies while hunting for sustenance: the snowmobile is a modern technology that serves to enhance the cultural practice of hunting, making it more productive and efficient within Cree cultural precepts.

I have my own example of interaction with the modern world and technology from my experience as an Indigenous publisher. I sometimes think websites might be the best medium for publishing some aspects of Oral Traditions. Some Traditional Stories are told only during certain seasons: some are told only in summer, some only in winter. They are not to be told outside that season. A website could present season-sensitive stories because it could be managed to respect the Protocol—so Winter Stories would only appear in winter, and so on. This solution would use a modern "untraditional" technology to respectfully extend Oral Traditions in the present and connect them to the future. It would be "untraditional" in the world of book publishing, too.

Here's another example: Mary Cardinal Collins, a contributor to this guide, has helped with a project on Facebook to identify Indigenous individuals in historical photographs. The photographs go up on a page, and people are asked to help with names and origins. Again, this is work in the present that uses a modern technology to bridge the past and the future. It is an expression of Indigenous cultural integrity and continuity.

Diversity and distinctness

Indigenous Peoples in what is now Canada have some cultural principles in common—such as principles of cultural adaption. They have some history in common—arising, for example, from their trading networks stretching back millennia and from their recent colonization by Europeans.

They comprise, however, many distinct societies that have distinct histories, languages, cultures, and identities. In general, they do not mind terms that are respectfully plural while grouping them together, such as *Indigenous Peoples*. It is even better, as much as possible, to speak of them as the separate entities that they are, with the specific words for their identity as they themselves express it.

PRINCIPLE 4: RECOGNIZING INDIGENOUS IDENTITY

Indigenous style recognizes that Indigenous Peoples view themselves according to the following key principles:

- They are diverse, distinct cultures.
- They exist as part of an ongoing continuum through the generations tracing back to their ancient ancestors.
- They have not been assimilated into mainstream Canadian society, and their national and cultural paradigms have not been fundamentally altered or undermined through colonization.
- They are currently in a process of cultural reclamation and

rejuvenation, marked by significant participation from Indigenous youth.

- Natural cultural change and adaptation do not mean that Indigenous Peoples have acquiesced to mainstream Canadian society, nor that Indigenous cultures have been fundamentally altered or undermined.

Case study: *Celia's Song*

Celia's Song, by Lee Maracle, was published in 2014 by Cormorant Books. This case study presents the perspectives of Lee Maracle, and her editor and publisher, on their working relationship.

LEE MARACLE, AUTHOR

In addition to Celia's Song, *her sixth and most-recent novel, Lee Maracle, who is Sto:Loh,* has also written three works of nonfiction and two books of poetry. She currently teaches at the Centre for Indigenous Studies at the University of Toronto.*

Indigenous authors have a different sense of what is important and significant. Some editors miss this: they'll take something internal to a paragraph and put it at the front. And then the paragraph says something different.

If that happens to too many paragraphs, then I know the editor doesn't get me: they don't know how my mind works. That's because they have a different point of view. That's when I think to myself that not very many non-Indigenous editors have worked on very many Indigenous books.

I trust Indigenous editors. I think it's maybe because they tell stories the way I do, so I kind of know what they'll accept or not. They edit for clarity. If it's clear, then fine: they leave it.

When you're introducing something—I'm talking as a writer now—the first line is always the most significant. It's the point you're making. It's there on purpose. Indigenous writing is about writing from the centre to the edge, to create a circle. We don't say things in

---

* This spelling follows the preference of Lee Maracle. Another spelling for this Indigenous People, which appears in this book, is Stô:Lō.

a linear way. We have long sentences and we grocery-list things with lots of semicolons. Editors with a European frame of mind, when they read that kind of writing, react that there are too many things running around in their heads. There aren't too many things for me. It's all connected to the first line and wraps up with the last line in a wheel of understanding. To put something into "Eurostructure," I have to find a way of breaking it down into a line-by-line linear map. I'll do that in some cases, but if something has gone on for ten thousand years, I'm not changing the way we say that.

Some people don't know how to edit me. I feel like, "If I accommodate you, I'm off track with what I need to say. If I don't accommodate you, I'm off track with what you're saying I need to say." There's no winning in that situation. It feels a bit like bullying.

The most courteous thing to do, if you're an editor, is to ask: "Why is this idea at the beginning of the paragraph?" Then, we can get into a discussion about that.

When I worked with Marc Côté on *Celia's Song*, he hadn't done a lot of Indigenous work. But he has a different sensitivity. The things he pulled out of my paragraphs were important to my thinking. For sure, he knows a lot about the West Coast—he grew up in Lynn Valley in North Vancouver, near where I grew up. So he knows something about us. I think he went to school with my younger brother.

Marc had known he wanted to edit a book of mine for some time before he worked on *Celia's Song*. He's a responsible publisher who, as a Canadian, needed to know who these Indigenous people are and bothered to find out.

We had a give-and-take relationship, an equal relationship. We were both interested in getting the best book possible. Marc assured me all the way through, paragraph by paragraph, that if I didn't want to change something, that was fine.

Marc and I had lots of conversations about how I write. Some of it's just my way of writing. Some of it is cultural. He knew his work began with trying to understand.

MARC CÔTÉ, PUBLISHER

I think the first time I encountered Lee was in January 1990, when the Ontario Arts Council [OAC] held a "Native Sounding." As the program assistant, twenty-nine years old, and only one month into the job, I was asked on no notice to handle the meeting for the OAC. The sounding was sixty "Native" writers gathered together to find out how the OAC could better accommodate them. Among the group were Lenore Keeshig-Tobias (as she was then), Basil Johnston, and, I think, Lee. I said that I wanted the meeting to run how was best for the sixty writers. Someone—I think it was Basil—suggested I leave the room for thirty minutes. When I returned, Lenore said, "You will be our scribe. All you will do is write down what we say." I agreed. I took about fifty pages of notes that day. All I did was listen—listen to hear exactly what was being said.

I learned a fundamental fact: Indigenous Peoples do not look at the world the same way as Europeans. They have more to teach the settler population than the settler population ever had to teach them. They have lived on this continent without destroying the land—something Europeans haven't figured out on two continents now. I learned hundreds of other facts, but nothing so important. (I got raves for the report. It was duly shelved and none of the recommendations ever saw the light of day.)

Lee brought *Celia's Song* to me in 2010. I read it and thought, "Oh, my. It's very Indigenous." We talked about writing "European Indigenous" like Joseph Boyden. Lee said, "I want to write like Lee Maracle, but I want to be read like Joseph Boyden." So there was my work cut out for me: her vision and voice, accessible to a large, European-educated audience.

The job of editing, as I understand it, is to work with the author. I worked with Lee the way I work with every Cormorant author. Every author is unique, as is every manuscript. I don't approach any manuscript as "genre fiction," not even a murder mystery. That might be the key to why Lee and I worked well together, and why *Celia's Song* is seen as a novel that retains its Indigeneity.

When we were working on the last portion of the book, Lee's articulation of West Coast Indigenous justice, I said, "You know. This reads like Freud's steps in analysis." She said—and this is a direct quotation—"I've heard of Freud, but I'm too busy to read him." It's not just me. At the Small Press Book Fair in Toronto in 2016, a woman walked by the Cormorant table, and said she was teaching *Celia's Song* at the University of Toronto and was astonished by the clear parallels between Freud's steps in analysis and Lee Maracle's articulation of West Coast Indigenous justice.

There were several times when I raised things that Lee disagreed with. One time I said, "This is redundant." "No it isn't, Marc." "Yes it is, Lee." "No it's not." And then I explained how the section read to me as redundant. She listened and then explained why it wasn't. Indigenous writing contains elements of storytelling that appear repetitious to a non-Indigenous mind, but which are not repetition. We heard each other and, as a result, we made very careful changes.

Another time, most notably, I thought that the man who abuses and rapes the little girl ought to be white. Lee said, "No. He has to be Indigenous." I asked why and she said, "Do I really have to tell you?" and I said, "Yes." So Lee explained, I listened, and I agreed.

4

The cultural rights of Indigenous Peoples

Cultural rights are part of contemporary Indigenous cultural realities. Understanding these rights, including how they evolved, is key to working in a culturally appropriate and respectful way.

Indigenous Peoples think of Creation as something that includes and sustains all living things. People are part of it and responsible for caring for it. The question of "who owns it" has no context.

By contrast, "who owns it" preoccupies European notions of the world. Consider, for example, that every bit of land in what is now Canada has some sort of ownership designation. Individuals own it, or corporations own it, or towns, or the Crown, and so on. If something isn't "owned"—air, for example—European notions consider it either free for the taking (mostly without value) or not yet owned.

Indigenous Peoples have formulated a new idea of ownership—Indigenous cultural property—to assert their place in a postcontact world of owned things. The Kainai used this idea in 1998 to repatriate Sacred Medicine Bundles from the Glenbow Museum in Calgary. The Haida used it in 2003 to repatriate the remains of ancestors from the Field Museum in Chicago. In 2017, it was at the centre of a successful online petition by Métis law student Jesse Donovan to repatriate Louis Riel's crucifix, knife, book of poetry, and clothing from the RCMP Heritage Centre in Regina, where Riel was executed, to the Métis Nation in Manitoba.

The concept of Indigenous cultural property also informs political commitments, such as the UN Declaration on the Rights of Indigenous Peoples and Australia's policies on using Indigenous cultural material.

The UN Declaration on the Rights of Indigenous Peoples

The General Assembly of the United Nations adopted the UN Declaration on the Rights of Indigenous Peoples (UNDRIP) on September 13, 2007. The declaration grew from many years of work and negotiation on the part of Indigenous Peoples around the world.

The declaration, though not binding, holds moral force as an international agreement and sets paramount ethical standards.

Article 31 concerns Indigenous cultural property. It says:

1. Indigenous peoples have the right to maintain, control, protect and develop their cultural heritage, traditional knowledge and traditional cultural expressions, as well as the manifestations of their sciences, technologies and cultures, including human and genetic resources, seeds, medicines, knowledge of the properties of fauna and flora, oral traditions, literatures, designs, sports and traditional games and visual and performing arts. They also have the right to maintain, control, protect and develop their intellectual property over such cultural heritage, traditional knowledge, and traditional cultural expressions.

2. In conjunction with indigenous peoples, States shall take effective measures to recognize and protect the exercise of these rights.[12]

Canada and the UN Declaration

Canada was one of the four UN member states that voted against UNDRIP at the UN General Assembly in 2007 (it also voted against

UNDRIP at the General Assembly in 2006). Canada issued a "statement of support" in 2010, which was careful to point out that the declaration did not change international or Canadian law regarding the rights of Indigenous Peoples.

In 2015, Prime Minister Justin Trudeau identified implementing the declaration as a task for his new government.

In 2016, Canada announced that it supported the declaration "without qualification." At the UN, Canada's Minister of Indigenous and Northern Affairs, Carolyn Bennett, said:

> [T]hrough Section 35 of its constitution, Canada has a robust framework for the protection of Indigenous rights. Section 35 of our constitution states, "the existing Aboriginal and treaty rights of Aboriginal peoples of Canada are hereby recognized and affirmed." . . .
>
> By adopting and implementing the declaration, we are excited that we are breathing life into Section 35 and recognizing it now as a full box of rights for Indigenous Peoples in Canada. Canada believes that our constitutional obligations serve to fulfill all of the principles of the declaration, including "free, prior and informed consent." We see modern treaties and self-government agreements as the ultimate expression of free, prior and informed consent among partners.[13]

So far, however, Canada has not formulated any specific policies about Indigenous cultural rights.

The example of Australia

Unlike Canada, and perhaps uniquely in the world, Australia has had detailed Indigenous cultural policies in since 2007, dating before UNDRIP.

The policies attach to the Australia Council for the Arts, which is an arts-funding body of the Australian government. They are protocols for using Indigenous cultural material in media arts, visual arts, performing arts, music, and writing.

The writing protocol quotes earlier work in Australia as foundational, including:

> Artists, writers and performers should refrain from incorporating

elements derived from Indigenous heritage into their works without the informed consent of the Indigenous owners.[14]

And:

Indigenous cultural and intellectual property rights refer to Indigenous people's rights to their cultural heritage. Heritage comprises all objects, sites and knowledge—the nature or use of which has been transmitted or continues to be transmitted from generation to generation, and which is regarded as pertaining to a particular Indigenous group or its territory.

Indigenous people's heritage is a living heritage and includes objects, knowledge, artistic, literary, musical and performance works, which may be created now or in the future, and based on that heritage.

Indigenous cultural and intellectual property rights include the right to:

- own and control Indigenous cultural and intellectual property
- ensure that any means of protecting Indigenous cultural and intellectual property is based on the principle of self-determination
- be recognised as the primary guardians and interpreters of their cultures
- authorise or refuse to authorise the commercial use of Indigenous cultural and intellectual property according to customary law
- maintain the secrecy of Indigenous knowledge and other cultural practices
- full and proper attribution
- control the recording of cultural customs and expressions, as well as the particular language that may be intrinsic to cultural identity, knowledge, skill, and teaching of culture.[15]

Taking its lead from this work, Australia's writing protocol details a framework for respecting Indigenous cultural property. Key elements of the framework include Indigenous control of content; community consultation and consent; respect for confidentiality; correct attribution and copyright; and correct distribution of royalties. It would be great if Canada, like Australia, articulated policies for respecting Indigenous cultural property—even greater if Indigenous cultural property were recognized in legislation, such as Canada's copyright act.

In the meantime, editors and publishers, as individuals and companies, can take steps themselves to do what is right.

PRINCIPLE 5: INDIGENOUS CULTURAL PROPERTY
Indigenous style involves publishing practices that recognize and respect Indigenous cultural property.

5

Culturally appropriate publishing practices for Indigenous authors and content

Working in a culturally appropriate way involves showing respect for Indigenous cultural Protocols and values, both in the work process and on the page.

Showing respect does not come from following rules. This chapter won't tell you "what to do" so you can jump through hoops and check the "did it" box. There is no single, cookbook way to do Indigenous publishing, because Indigenous Peoples are diverse. Indigenous publishing is about finding your way through, grounded in respect for Indigenous ways of being in the world and for Indigenous Peoples as distinct from one another.

Finding your way through requires thought, care, attention, and dialogue. It requires working with people. It requires the engagement and inclusion needed for a new conversation between Indigenous Peoples and settler society.

Collaborate

The key to working in a culturally appropriate way is to collaborate with the Indigenous Peoples at the centre of a work. Collaboration ensures that works do not speak *for* Indigenous Peoples. It ensures that works *are* Indigenous Peoples *speaking*. Only Indigenous Peoples speak with the authority of who they are, connected to Traditional Knowledge, their Oral Traditions, their cultural Protocols, and their contemporary identity. Collaboration is crucial in achieving authentic content, and in demonstrating respect for the complexity and individual nature of Indigenous Peoples.

PRINCIPLE 6: COLLABORATION

Work in collaboration with Indigenous Peoples and authors to ensure that Indigenous material is expressed with the highest possible level of cultural authenticity, and in a manner that follows Indigenous Protocols and maintains Indigenous cultural integrity.

MAKE THE CIRCLE OF COLLABORATION OPEN

Allow the process of collaboration to include a large circle of Indigenous contributors.

Indigenous information, generally, is not "standardized." It comes from the experience and expression of particular Indigenous Peoples and individuals. Knowing where information comes from—the source community, the source individual—is an important aspect of Indigenous cultural continuity.

So, Indigenous publishing often involves consulting and acknowledging many people.

TAKE THE NECESSARY TIME

That takes time. Do your best to take the time.

Case study: Indigenous and non-Indigenous authors in collaboration

Speaking from their extensive experience, Sophie McCall and Deanna Reder present their perspectives on working collaboratively.

Sophie McCall is a Scottish-descended settler scholar who teaches Indigenous and Canadian literatures at Simon Fraser University (SFU).

Deanna Reder is a Cree-Métis* scholar who teaches in the departments of First Nations Studies and English at SFU.

SOPHIE MCCALL

Collaboration has profoundly shaped the format, intellectual directions, outcomes, and most importantly the process by which I have pursued my research and writing. I feel honoured that I have had the opportunity to work collaboratively with Indigenous colleagues, writers, artists, and scholars on a variety of projects.

The *Oxford English Dictionary* defines *collaboration* in two ways: "1) The action of working with someone to produce something; and 2) Traitorous cooperation with an enemy." Both senses of the word are true and important to bear in mind. Collaboration, in the sense of working together with others to produce projects, is one way to counter the history of representing Indigenous Peoples by non-Indigenous authors, who often did not consult with or seek consent from the communities they studied. Collaborations often require years to complete and universities can provide a "home" during long periods of gestation and production. Universities' granting agencies, libraries, archives, and spaces for meeting provide material support that can facilitate work with independent artists, who require adequate recompense for their work. However, those very same institutional structures perpetuate power relationships that shape the interactions between collaborators. One voice can become dominant. What begins as "collaboration" can, in the worst-case scenario, devolve into "appropriation." In acknowledging the larger political contexts of the work I do, I find that the Janus-faced definition of collaboration captures an ever-present paradox of resistance and complicity that I must navigate.

My work with Métis interdisciplinary artist Gabrielle L'Hirondelle

---

* This spelling follows the preference of Deanna Reder.

Hill, who was my primary collaborator and coeditor on *The Land We Are: Artists and Writers Unsettle the Politics of Reconciliation* (ARP, 2015), convinced me that collaboration does not have to aim for a seamless platform of agreement; indeed, collaboration can embrace differences and acknowledge conflict. We came to think of our process as one of working across differences of experience, profession, background, and interests. Each chapter of *The Land We Are* is collaboratively authored, and includes the contributors' self-reflections on collaboration. Working with people takes time, and sometimes we were attracted to shortcuts as deadlines loomed. As we pulled the chapters together into a book, Gabrielle and I often used Track Changes to efficiently convey editing suggestions to contributors. When Tsimshian/Cree multimedia artist Skeena Reece asked that we print her chapter (coauthored by settler artist Sandra Semchuk) with the Track Changes edits visible, we felt exposed, caught in our own game, before realizing the brilliance of this request. Gabrielle and I had intervened into an intimate conversation between Reece and Semchuk; thus we must avow our presence in that conversation. To this day, that chapter, more than any other, sparks questions and comments from readers.

Cree-Métis scholar Deanna Reder is a key collaborator, colleague, and friend; even more, she is a mentor, and she has taught me virtually everything I know about how to build successful collaborations across differences. She has a long list of collaborative projects, most notably a five-year project, "The People and the Text," which aims to build a collaborative literary history of multigenre Indigenous texts published up to 1992. She has thought a great deal about practising Indigenous methods of reading, interpreting, and editing texts, and honouring tribally specific Intellectual Traditions and Protocols. In her scholarly writings, the Cree word for kinship, *wâhkotowin*, is a key concept: building kinship relationships has become the basis of her approach to collaboration. I have included a short excerpt from a conversation we had, in which we discussed what collaboration means to her and the key ingredients in building successful collaborative relationships.

Deanna Reder: I think of the words of Cree intellectual Harold Cardinal. The search for knowledge in the Four Worlds gives us the idea that Indigenous research is done from one generation to another. No one person is going to do it all; no one generation is going to do it all.

You can't decide to yourself, "Oh, I am going to collaborate with that group over there and boy are they lucky." (Laughs) You have to instead really focus on establishing the basic groundwork of whatever it is you might have to offer. And then you must wait for those relationships to unfold. I don't really even like knocking on doors. You have to let people know that you're willing, and try to be ready when they're ready.

I will give you a perfect example. In 2006, in my last year of grad school, I had the privilege to see a play by dramatherapist Vera Manuel, daughter of Secwepemc political leader George Manuel and Ktunaxa community worker Marceline Paul. The play was produced in Vancouver by the Helping Spirit Lodge Society and when I went to speak to its director, Geni Manuel, I discovered that she was Vera's niece. It was in that conversation that Geni gave me several unpublished plays that her association had put together under Vera's direction. I really wanted to do something with these plays for a long, long time, but was overwhelmed when I began my new job in 2007 and by my uncertainty about what to do with them. At the same time, I was working with Métis scholar Jo-Ann Episkenew and Algonquin scholar Michelle Coupal. At one point, Jo-Ann gave Michelle a photocopy of the only play Vera had ever published, in 1986, which had fallen out of print: *Strength of Indian Women* about residential school experiences. Jo-Ann insisted: "You've got to teach this." In a later conversation, Michelle told me, "We've got to get this play back into publication," and I realized that this was the chance to work together with her on the plays entrusted to me several years previously. This itself was an amazing chance to work together, but then, a few months later, we bumped into Joanne Arnott, a Métis poet I've known for years, only to discover that, in the last year of Vera's life, Joanne had begun curating a collection of Vera's poetry. At first it was a shock. Michelle and I immediately recognized that we as academics had a lot more access to publishing and power. What could we do to support a project directed by an independent poet? And then of course it just seemed obvious: we should work together. This snowballed when we connected with Vera's sister, Emalene, who had saved Vera's archive. Imagine our sense of wonder when we came across some of Vera's stories that were written in 1988, stories that are drop-dead gorgeous, needing practically no editing. And suddenly what was going to be "The Plays and Poetry of Vera Manuel" became "The Plays, Stories, and Poetry of Vera

Manuel." The title of the volume, due in 2018, is *Honouring the Strength of Indian Women*.

Sophie McCall: The theme here seems to be that you feel that successful collaborations must involve serendipitous connections between people. Because you can't just say, "Here I am in this position, with funding and institutional support, and I am just going to go ahead with my project." Sometimes the zeitgeist is not there.

Deanna Reder: It's both the benefit and the danger of working within the university system: we have a lot more access to publishing and to funding. We have opportunities all the time, much more than community members normally have. But all along we're navigating pretty significant trip wires. You don't want to be in any way taking over, because it's really Vera's legacy and it's her sister, Emalene, who's been guarding that legacy. It's disingenuous to imagine yourself as not powerful. But it doesn't mean you can't be involved as an ally.

I take very seriously the work of Margaret Kovach, the Cree educational researcher and author of *Indigenous Methodologies*. She's the only author I can think of who actually asks you to think about the work you do in the context of your own life's purpose. This is something we never think about in the university context. Her advice is: do the projects that work toward your larger goals or your life work. You can say no to projects that don't make sense to you.

Follow Indigenous Protocols

Protocols are appropriate ways of using cultural material, and of interacting with Indigenous Peoples and Indigenous communities. They encourage ethical conduct and promote interaction based on good faith and mutual respect.[16]

Indigenous Protocols are an important aspect of complex traditional systems of Indigenous governance. The languages and cultures of Indigenous Peoples across Canada and around the world have transmitted Protocols through time. Although these systems of knowledge have been disrupted, throughout the generations people have maintained and protected these ways of working and being together.[17]

I want to make a note about word choice and style here. *Protocols* is a better word than *customs* for these systems of knowledge. *Customs* implies something less formal than what Protocols are. The word

Protocols is capitalized as a way to mark the permanence and significance of these systems of knowledge as Indigenous institutions. You can also call Protocols *Indigenous Laws.*

Indigenous editing and publishing are about transmitting information. Doing this properly involves, in particular, Protocols that observe respect for Elders and Oral Traditions. Indigenous Peoples are diverse and there is no single set of Protocols that work for all communities. Part of the need to "find your way through" comes from respecting that diversity.

Observing respect for Elders

As an editor, publisher, or writer—especially if you are non-Indigenous, but also if you are Indigenous and working outside your own cultural context—you may need to find someone who can give authentic information about an Indigenous People. Sometimes that person is an Elder, particularly if the information involves Traditional Knowledge or Oral Traditions.

How do you know when to approach Elders? How do you find Elders? The best way is to ask someone from the Indigenous People you are seeking to understand. For the most part, First Nations, Inuit, and Métis people do not expect you, as someone outside their culture, to know who their Elders are or when consulting Elders is called for. Asking for help is not disrespectful and is always a good step.

I have already talked about the internal cultural imperatives of Indigenous Peoples, and the ultimate responsibility of the current generation to be the link between the ancestors and future generations. Elders, especially, assume this ultimate responsibility, which requires knowledge, vision, observation, synthesis, and communication.

OFFER A GIFT OF RESPECT

Gifts of respect are an important part of Protocols with Elders.

You usually need to approach Elders individually with a gift of respect. Tobacco is often a safe choice, but not always. Again, ask for help. You can ask the Elder herself or himself: "I would like to offer you a gift of respect. What gift would be appropriate?" You can also ask around the community to see what an Elder might like. Tlicho* author Richard Van Camp tells of tracking down a limited edition of the *Chippewa Dictionary* that he knew an Elder really wanted. Richard was so pleased to find it, and the Elder appreciated that special gift.

GET TO KNOW THE ELDERS

Another important part of Protocols around Elders is getting to know Elders (so they can get to know you, too). This means spending time with them—in person is best—and talking with them about your project. Say what you're going to ask their testimony for. Are you checking the accuracy of something you think is part of Traditional Knowledge? Does what you seek perhaps involve the Oral Tradition? How will you use the testimony? Is it for a textbook? Is it for a memoir? Or something else?

LISTEN

Then, listen to what you are told. Listen to the significance of the stories and knowledge. It comes from the ancestors through thousands of years.

EXTEND RIGHT OF REVIEW

Let the Elders know that they will see your project before it is published and will have an opportunity to comment. Use their comments.

PRINCIPLE 7: ELDERS

Indigenous style recognizes the significance of Elders in the cultural integrity of Indigenous Peoples and as authentic sources of Indigenous cultural information.

Indigenous style follows Protocols to observe respect for Elders.

---

* This follows a spelling used by Richard Van Camp.

Observing respect for Traditional Knowledge and Oral Traditions

Traditional Knowledge and Oral Traditions should be part of our lives as human beings. They are living parts of the world's cultures. All of us should be curious about them. All of us would be better for learning about them and from them.

Traditional Knowledge and Oral Traditions, however, are Indigenous cultural property, owned by the Indigenous Peoples they come from. Like any property, no one has the *right* to use them except their owners. Everyone else must seek permission to use them.

This is perhaps a difficult notion in the context of conventional publishing, which revolves around individual authorship of textual works. Traditional Knowledge and Oral Traditions have no individual authors, and sometimes have no textual form. But that does not mean they are free for the taking, even if the letter of European-inspired law does not yet recognize Indigenous cultural property.

PRINCIPLE 8: WORKING WITH TRADITIONAL KNOWLEDGE AND ORAL TRADITIONS

Indigenous style recognizes Traditional Knowledge and Oral Traditions as Indigenous cultural property, owned by Indigenous Peoples and over which Indigenous Peoples exert control. This recognition has bearing on permission and copyright, and applies even when non-Indigenous laws do not require it.

Writers, editors, and publishers should make every effort to ensure that Indigenous Protocols are followed in the publication of Traditional Knowledge and Oral Traditions. Where culturally sensitive Indigenous materials are in question, writers, editors, and publishers should make every effort to consult an authoritative member of the particular Indigenous People for confirmation.

SEEK CONSENT

Consent must come from the Indigenous People the Traditional Knowledge and Oral Tradition comes from.

Consent may flow through the trust you place in an author, whom you have come to know, or it may come from consulting the Elders of that Indigenous People.

If for some reason—perhaps the context is a project that seeks to republish content from an earlier work—you cannot identify the Indigenous People that owns a Traditional Story or a practice from Traditional Knowledge, do not use that content. You do not have permission.

ALWAYS COLLABORATE

Use extreme caution in editing and publishing Traditional Knowledge, especially in editing and publishing Indigenous Oral Traditions. Indigenous collaboration and consultation should be sought in all such cases. This is an area where Indigenous editors are very useful.

As a publisher or editor, be prepared to find out during the process of collaboration that, in some cases, it is not appropriate to publish Traditional Knowledge and Oral Traditions.

DO NOT PUBLISH IN BREACH OF PROTOCOLS

The Protocols of Traditional Knowledge and Oral Traditions mean that not everything they contain is appropriate for book publishing. Traditional Knowledge contains information about medicines and herbology that has sacred significance. Oral Traditions contain Sacred Stories. Other stories can only be told by certain families or Clans, or only by women or men, or only during certain seasons.

Indigenous Peoples are very offended when publishing breaches the Protocols of Traditional Knowledge and Oral Traditions. It is a violation that echoes colonial attitudes. As Jo-ann Archibald says: "Losing 'the eyes,' or understanding, of a worldview embedded in Aboriginal oral traditions . . . is strongly linked to the legacy of forced colonization and assimilation during the missionary and residential-school eras and through the public school system (Archibald 1993; Ashworth 1979; Battiste 2000; Haig-Brown 1988; Kirkness 1981; Royal Commission on Aboriginal Peoples 1996b)."[18]

CHECK ALREADY-PUBLISHED INDIGENOUS CONTENT

There are many examples of non-Indigenous anthropologists during the 1960s, 1970s, and 1980s publishing collections from Oral Traditions in breach of Protocols. It's important to know this, so you don't republish all or parts of these works without first seeking advice.

Just because it's in a book—or especially if it's in an academic book from the 1960s, 1970s, and 1980s—doesn't mean the content was appropriate to publish in the first place, or that it has been published with consent, or that it has been published accurately.

In the past, Indigenous cultural material has been subject to interpretation by non-Indigenous people. Today, as Indigenous Peoples seek to reclaim control over their cultural property, Indigenous interpretation is a way of enhancing the cultural significance of the content.[19]

ASSIGN COPYRIGHT CORRECTLY

In mainstream publishing, the copyright of a work is generally held by the author—the person who "writes it." But a person who "writes down" Traditional Knowledge or Oral Traditions is not their author.

Traditional Knowledge and Oral Traditions are the cultural property of the Indigenous People they come from. It doesn't matter who "wrote it down." The copyright should be held by that Indigenous People. Works that contain aspects of Traditional Knowledge should include an acknowledgement of Indigenous collaboration and consultation, and of the Indigenous Peoples who are the sources of the knowledge.

Writers should not claim authorship over Traditional Knowledge. This applies to Indigenous authors, too, even if they have followed Protocols. The Indigenous press I work for, Theytus Books, never takes copyright for content from Traditional Knowledge or Oral Traditions. Its practice is to ask authors to consider—if their book is all from an Oral Tradition or from Traditional Knowledge—whether their name should appear as author. As a publisher or editor, you should suggest their name should appear in the context of "as told by" or "as transcribed by" or "as interpreted through."

Sometimes the *entire* work of an author does not rest on Traditional Knowledge or Oral Traditions, but only *parts*. For example, an author may incorporate aspects of Traditional Knowledge or excerpts from an Oral Tradition. For those parts, copyright still rests with the source Indigenous People. Magadala Books, an Indigenous publisher in Australia, has suggested, in these cases, negotiating terms to use the content through a licensing arrangement:

> Most Aboriginal stories are part of an oral tradition and have never been written down. If someone wishes to record a story (by writing it down or taping it) then the recorder could claim to be the copyright owner of the material because they are the one who has written it down. A way to control this would be for the storyteller to argue that, as the story is theirs, the recorder should assign in writing the copyright back to the storyteller, who can then license the recorder to use the material in certain specified ways, such as for research or for linguistic work.[20]

DO NOT ASSUME PUBLIC DOMAIN

Conventional publishing assigns a time limit on the rights of authors. For example, in Canada, generally, a work becomes part of the public domain fifty years after the author's death. So, at that point, the work is literally free for the taking under Canadian law.

Time limits like this don't apply to Indigenous cultural property. Indigenous Peoples own their Traditional Knowledge and Oral Histories in perpetuity.

Let's say a missionary in 1880 wrote down a Traditional Story of an Indigenous People and then included it in his memoir. The memoir, by Canadian law, would now be in the public domain. The Traditional Story, by Indigenous Protocol, would not. You shouldn't use the Traditional Story without consent from the Indigenous People who (still and always) own it.

Case study: Kou-skelowh series and *River of Salmon Peoples*

This case study presents two examples of publishing projects from Theytus Books that have followed Indigenous publishing principles. These projects are particularly important in their approach to Oral Traditions.

The first example—the Kou-skelowh series—predates me as publisher at Theytus Books. The second—*River of Salmon Peoples*—involved me after the initial process of consultation had taken place.

KOU-SKELOWH/WE ARE THE PEOPLE: A TRILOGY OF OKANAGAN LEGENDS*

The Kou-skelowh series comprises three children's books that present Traditional Okanagan Legends translated into English and accompanied by illustrations. One of the most valuable aspects of the Kou-skelowh series was the process of its development—what it regarded as proper publishing practices for Indigenous cultural material.

In 1981, on behalf of Theytus, Jeannette Armstrong asked the Okanagan Elders Council for permission to publish some Traditional Legends. The Elders gave permission to publish three legends. Armstrong translated the three legends into English. Armstrong and Theytus then took the English versions to the Elders Council for examination, and made revisions until the Elders Council approved the legends for educational use by Okanagan children.

Theytus then asked the Elders Council for permission to publish the legends for sale in the book trade. After lengthy discussions, Theytus was granted permission with several conditions. A key condition was that no individual would claim ownership of the legends or benefit from the sales. Theytus also asked the Elders Council to name the series. They chose *Kou-skelowh*, meaning "we are the people."

Theytus published the original Kou-skelowh series in 1984. It published the most recent version of the series in 1991. The

---

* The name used here for the Indigenous People involved in this project follows the name current at the time of the project, which is also the name that appears in the published work.

series has no author: on the cover and the copyright page, each book acknowledges its origins with the statement "An Okanagan Legend." Okanagan Tribal Council holds the copyright of the series, and receives royalty payments, which was another condition of permission from the Elders Council.

RIVER OF SALMON PEOPLES

This project involved two-and-a-half years of consultation with most of the Indigenous communities along the Fraser River from Prince George to Seabird Island. The consultations started in 2009 and the book was published in 2015.

The consultation happened through workshops that were set up in collaboration with individual communities. The workshops involved Elders, youth, artists, fishers, and community leaders sharing ancient and contemporary information.

The book lists more than 130 contributors.

The information took a variety of forms: songs, dances, visual media, and recitations of contemporary stories and Traditional Stories. It documented the relationship of Peoples to the salmon and to each other through the salmon. The purpose of the workshops was to transcribe the information for publication.

The project hired a team of Indigenous writers and designers to identify organizing themes for the book from the materials gathered at the workshops.

As the editor's introduction says, "It was clear from the beginning of the process that this book project was not to come from a place of academia, or political, historical, sociological or anthropological positions."

Copyright for this work is held by ten Indigenous Peoples, who are listed on the copyright page: Nak'azdli, Secwepemc, Stô:Lō, Sta'at'imc, Musqueam, Lil'wat7ul, Nle'kepmxcin, Tsilhqot'in, Dakelh, and Syilx.*

Know the importance of relationship

Putting Traditional Knowledge and Oral Traditions into textual form underscores the need for a context of relationship and trust in Indigenous publishing.

---

* These names follow spellings derived in consultation with the Indigenous Peoples who authored *River of Salmon Peoples*.

As a publisher or editor, Indigenous or not, you can't just "get someone to sign off" on Indigenous content from Traditional Knowledge and Oral Traditions.

Traditional Knowledge and Oral Traditions can form part of many kinds of works, both fiction and nonfiction. In nonfiction, the inclusion of content from Traditional Knowledge and Oral Traditions can be obvious, which can make the need to follow Protocols obvious. Not always, though: a memoir might touch on this content as part of recollection or family history. Fiction is perhaps a more complicated context: the Indigenous Voice, for example, involves combining and extending Traditional Knowledge and Oral Traditions with new ideas and expressions.

This means you need to have trust in the person writing the work. You need to trust that they have followed Protocols, and built the relationships that allow them to share the knowledge or tell the story. Trusting the author means getting to know the author. It's about relationship. In Indigenous publishing, you have to build your trust out of relationship, not just out of a contract.

The Indigenous cultural imperatives of truthfulness, honesty, mindfulness about community impacts, and continuity with history and heritage apply to everyone working to write, edit, and publish Indigenous content.

PRINCIPLE 9: THE ROLE OF RELATIONSHIP AND TRUST
Indigenous style recognizes the essential role of relationship and trust in producing works with authentic Indigenous content, and the source of relationship and trust in truthfulness, honesty, mindfulness about community impacts, and continuity with history and heritage.

Who benefits from Indigenous content?

In the history of publishing Indigenous content by non-Indigenous authors in Canada, it has been unusual for the Indigenous Peoples or individuals providing the content to receive compensation.

This is partly because conventional copyright does not recognize Indigenous cultural property, so revenues for using Traditional Knowledge and Oral Traditions have not, generally, flowed back to their owners in the form of royalties. Part of it may also come from a notion in conventional publishing that inclusion in a book is its own reward.

The contribution of Indigenous Peoples to publications creates wealth. Sharing the wealth is a matter of respect and fairness.

Royalties are important. So is direct compensation to individual Indigenous contributors. Collaboration places demands of time and personal expense on individual contributors. These demands are not insignificant, and are only likely to increase as Canadian publishing becomes more reconciliation-aware.

Indigenous style requires engagement with Indigenous Peoples, and Indigenous contributors should not be the only ones covering the costs.

PRINCIPLE 10: COMPENSATION

Indigenous style recognizes the importance of royalties to Indigenous Peoples and authors—and compensation to individual Indigenous contributors, and to Indigenous communities and organizations—as part of fair and respectful publishing relationships.

Case study: *Aboriginal Studies 10, 20*, and *30*

Aboriginal Studies 10, 20, and *30* were social studies textbooks for the Alberta curriculum published in 2004–2005 by Les Éditions Duval/Duval House Publishing. This project involved four Indigenous publishing partners, and more than fifty Indigenous contributors, writers, advisors, and validators from more than twenty Indigenous Nations in Alberta and other parts of Canada.

This case study presents perspectives from a contributor and the publisher on the project's publishing practices.

MARY CARDINAL COLLINS, CONTRIBUTOR

Mary Cardinal Collins is a semiretired teacher, and fluent Cree speaker and translator—nehiyaw-skwew—who has worked in the field of Indigenous languages and Indigenous education for more than thirty years.

I review a lot of books (I'm Plains Cree). I don't know of another textbook project that has invited people from the community to write.

In *Aboriginal Studies 10*, for example, I wrote a little piece about moose hunting. I asked the help of Cree Elder George Cardinal from Peerless Lake for words to describe moose. Cree has many specific words: *onîcaniw* is a female moose before giving birth; *oskoweskwanmotayew* is a four-year-old male moose. We choose nine examples in all. When something is important, Indigenous Peoples have many words to describe it. That's what the piece shows.

It's important to involve people. It's not any good to say, "This is how I do it." What is said has to come from inside the communities. This project had a lot of back and forth. It had input from many people. That's the way you have to do it. You can't just "pick somebody" to "write it." A lot of people have to be involved. That's the Indigenous way, because Indigenous Peoples have to own it.

You can see the names of the people who contributed to the book on the copyright page. The names are important because, without the names, you don't know where the information comes from. There's no continuity. It's good that *Aboriginal Studies* wrote all the names down.

It's important to present authentic information. Duval consulted, and fact-checked, and knew where to look for the authentic information. Instead of assuming something was true, or taking it from a book, they would call someone like me and ask, "What is this?"

Duval also knew their Ps and Qs about Protocol. They knew, for instance, that different groups might follow different Protocols in observing respect for Elders. Some might take tobacco, others might not. They sorted it out by asking. And they were open and welcoming.

It's important to respect the diversity of Indigenous Peoples. This project involved all the groups in Alberta and showed the diversity of Indigenous Peoples here.

That diversity sometimes made things complicated, and it was important to respect that. There's a place in *Aboriginal Studies 10* where we talk about communal ceremonies such as the *Dawats'ethe* of the Dené Tha' (the English for the dance is "Tea Dance"), the

Mâskisimowin of the Woodland Cree ("Round Dance"), and the *Pâhkwesimôwin* of the Plains Cree and *Akóka'tssin* of the Blackfoot Confederacy (both of these are "Sundances" in English). This section also talks about the Sweat Lodge. The editors wanted a kind of pictorial essay on the Sweat Lodge. But there are all kinds of styles for the Sweat Lodge that are valid for different Indigenous Peoples. A lot has to do with the direction the doorway faces, and how many doorways there are. So, the response to that idea was, "The Sweat Lodge is important, but we don't want to suggest it has a single style." People were concerned about the future, that young people in the future would point to this textbook and say, "That's the way a Sweat Lodge is built." So the book doesn't have a pictorial essay about the Sweat Lodge.

You have to take time to vet things. One time I was reading something on the Cree—I can't remember what it was—and there was a picture of my cousin! And it said he was a Medicine Man or a Chief. He isn't. He's a dancer. It takes time to vet things properly. You can't just slap a picture down. Research takes time. In *Aboriginal Studies*, we were careful to name and correctly describe the people in pictures. That kind of detail shows respect for who people are.

GLENN ROLLANS, PUBLISHER

Glenn Rollans was a partner in Les Éditions Duval/Duval House Publishing during the Aboriginal Studies project. He is now a partner in Brush Education, which has published this guide.

By the time we were contracted by Alberta Education to develop and publish the Aboriginal Studies series, Duval had already published well over one hundred Indigenous learning resources as non-Indigenous publishers in partnership with Indigenous communities, mostly language-learning, cultural, and health resources. Even so, this project retaught or emphasized three big lessons for me.

The first is to involve absolutely as many people as possible from the communities who will be your primary audiences. Most teachers and students, Indigenous and non-Indigenous, look at educational resources partly as a mirror: they want to see themselves reflected on the page before using and trusting the resource.

We had four main Indigenous publishing partners for the series: the Kainai Board of Education (located in Treaty 7 Territory), the Métis Nation of Alberta, the Northland School Division (located in Treaty 8), and the Tribal Chiefs Institute of Treaty 6. The listing of credits for this series stretches over two pages, and lists more than a hundred contributors, most of them representing our Indigenous partners on the project. You can't always build that big a team, but when you can, it's great.

The second lesson is that sharing the money needs more emphasis as part of a relationship of respect. The relationship between publisher and authors depends on both real respect and the tangible symbols of respect. Our partners and contributors each contributed themselves, their essence, to the essence of the books—they spoke for their communities and cultures, not us. So, they needed to be respected and rewarded. We entered into what resembled an author's contract with each of our publishing partners: each publishing partner had a ten percent royalty.

We asked ourselves, "How do we resource this so we can do it properly?" We knew that our work as publishers—we had only one year to create three full high-school textbooks with teacher's guides, start to finish—would eat up a lot of money. But we still built a business plan that committed forty percent of net sales to our partners. We negotiated more presales than we thought was possible, and together with our partners we created Alberta textbooks and teacher's guides that found audiences all across Canada. Alberta Education committed funds that made the project possible. Indian and Northern Affairs Canada actually asked to fund the teacher's guides. Again, you can't always do all this, but it's always the right goal.

Third, we learned again to listen, listen, listen. We wanted to do something genuinely created by a broad cross-section of Indigenous Peoples in Alberta. It was community authorship. With our Indigenous partners, we said, "What do you want to say about yourself?" And then we let the books speak with their words and embody their perspectives. We tried to be as perfect a conduit as we could be, adding value as publishers without subtracting.

You don't learn anything by talking instead of listening. You don't learn anything by being defensive. The conversation around colonialism assigns blame, and that can be uncomfortable for a non-Indigenous person involved in the conversation. You have to listen and accept your share.

You negotiate contentious issues through authentic relationships with other people. Building relationship involves time, respect plus outward indicators of respect, and people working with people, often face to face. You have to commit to all of those things.

The essence of it going well is: be a good listener, recognize the generosity of what others are doing, and be generous yourself.

And, as part of listening, don't expect credit or congratulations for doing your job properly. We're *supposed* to be an invisible profession. If you earn it, you'll get it, and those are wonderful moments.

6

Terminology

The goal of Indigenous style is to show respect for Indigenous ways of being the world in the publishing process and on the page.

The last chapter was about the publishing process. This chapter and the next are about the words on the page.

"Getting it right" in terms of words on the page can be difficult. The standard you have to meet as an editor or publisher is basically impossible: it is the standard of each reader, each with their particular context and their own identity. A lot of people would like to talk about Indigenous issues honestly and don't want to cause offence—they can get very stressed out about the proper terms.[21] In addition, the process of decolonizing language surrounding Indigenous Peoples is not finished: terms, names, and styles continue to evolve.

So, plan on not getting it right. Make your best effort to make informed, mindful choices about terminology.

This means, first and foremost, taking direction from the author or from the Indigenous People or Peoples at the centre of a work. It also means declaring your limitations as an arbiter of language: explain the choices and thought that inform the words on the page, in an editor's introduction, for example, or in footnotes; and acknowledge the place of different terminology in other Indigenous works.

Find your way through, and show how you have found your way through.

Inappropriate terms

Although some terminology surrounding Indigenous Peoples continues to evolve, some terminology is clearly *always* not right.

Just as words such as *negro* to describe African Americans and *man* or *mankind* to describe human civilization have fallen out of use because they are generally offensive to African Americans and women, there are many terms associated with Indigenous Peoples that require—at least—rethinking, and, in some cases, complete avoidance.

Chelsea Vowel states the following on inappropriate terminology: "Surprisingly, there are a great number of people who still think the use of some of these terms is up for debate, but I would sincerely like to help you avoid unintentionally putting your foot in your mouth. So, between us, let's just agree the following words are never okay to call Indigenous peoples: savage, red Indian, redskin, primitive, half-breed, squaw/brave/buck/papoose."[22]

This section reviews examples of questionable or culturally inappropriate terminology.

The origins of inappropriate terms

Many inappropriate terms stem from three main sources:

- **Explorer and missionary language.** The connotations of many terms derived from explorers and missionaries are generally biased by the ideas of conquest of territory and conversion of Indigenous Peoples to Christianity.
- **Anthropology and archaeology.** An entire lexicon of terminology commonly used in reference to Indigenous Peoples came out of the discipline of anthropology, and to a lesser extent, archaeology. Both disciplines tend to view Indigenous Peoples as remnants of the past, and many terms tend to denigrate

and dehumanize Indigenous Peoples. They have often presented Indigenous Peoples as "primitive" societies that should be documented before they inevitably develop into modern, Western-based peoples (i.e., "the vanishing race"). These precepts clearly go against the Indigenous cultural principle that Indigenous Peoples have vibrant, evolving cultures based on ancient fundamentals.

- **Kitsch terminology.** A lexicon of terminology used in reference to Indigenous Peoples can be traced to American and Canadian kitsch literature and filmmaking. This particular set of terminology is generally marked by vagueness, meaninglessness, and overt racism, and is thus often extremely offensive to Indigenous Peoples.

Works in each of these areas or genres borrow terminology from the others, and, in some cases, the common use of terms in a particular area has become accepted across the board.

It is also important to note that while many of these terms may be inappropriate or problematic, they are often still used (even by Indigenous Peoples). Many terms retain an ambiguous status as they are used habitually or because no alternate terminology has been proposed.

Examples of inappropriate and offensive terms

artifact: This term is commonly used in anthropology, archaeology, and art history to refer to artworks and functional objects produced by Indigenous Peoples. The etymological *Oxford English Dictionary* (OED) has two definitions for *artifact* relevant to its use for Indigenous cultural objects. The first is "an object made or modified by human workmanship, as opposed to one formed by natural processes." The second is specifically from archaeology: "an excavated object that shows characteristic signs of human workmanship or use." Both definitions are problematic in Indigenous contexts.

The first definition, when applied to Indigenous cultural materials, risks stripping the materials of their essential connection to specific Indigenous Peoples and their forms of expression. The second definition risks stripping them of their connection to the present: it can be interpreted to mean that ancient Indigenous artworks, for example, are remnants of the past and disassociated from the contemporary members of an Indigenous People.

When you see *artifact*, you are most likely looking at content that needs reworking and vetting. Consult the Indigenous People at the centre of the content, and ask them for the words to describe the purpose and significance of what is at issue. Do your best to be as specific as possible.

band: This term is commonly used to describe Indigenous groups in anthropology and was adopted, and is still used, by the Canadian government. The relevant OED definition of *band* is "a confederation of persons having a common purpose."

Compare this to OED's first definition of *nation*: "a large aggregate of communities and individuals united by factors such as common descent, language, culture, history, or occupation of the same territory, so as to form a distinct people."

Or compare it to this OED definition of *people*: "the body of men, women, and children comprising a particular nation, community, ethnic group, etc."

Here is an OED definition of *society*: "the aggregate of persons living together in a community, especially one having shared customs, laws, and institutions."

Band describes something looser than *nation*, *people*, or *society*. It does not specify political or national structure, or include historical, cultural, or territorial aspects of identity. It is therefore inappropriate to describe Indigenous Peoples, who have rich and ancient histories, cultural traditions, and governance systems. Despite its problems, *band* must in some cases be used because it is established in the Indian Act as the administrative body of a reserve and the collective as a whole. The colonizing Indian Act has also divided Indigenous Nations into bands, and encouraged Indigenous People to identify with their band.[23]

barbarian/barbarism: These terms were first used in explorer logs to denote Indigenous Peoples as lacking in cultural refinement. They carry connotations of "violent and unstructured peoples" with little or no social organization, and also have evolutionary connotations. The terms are obviously inappropriate to describe the hundreds of complex Indigenous societies and political institutions that adhered to such concepts as democracy and gender equality.

brave: An offensive term for an Indigenous man.

buck: An offensive term for a young Indigenous man.

clan: As a lowercase term, this has the same problems as *band*. It conveys loose, informal organization instead of structure, history, and purpose. As an uppercase term, *Clan* describes governance structures, such as the Clan System of the Haudenosaunee, which involves eight Clans that transcend, and so integrate, the individual nations of the Haudenosaunee Confederacy. This is an appropriate use. Many other Indigenous Nations also have Clan Systems, which are an important part of traditional governance, and social and spiritual organization.

discovery: This term, when used to describe European arrival in the Americas and other places occupied by Indigenous Peoples, literally implies that Indigenous Peoples did not exist as social beings with the capacity to occupy territory. It is erroneous and ethnocentric, but still commonly used in anthropological and historical texts. The legal counterpart to *discovery* is *terra nullius* (generally meaning "unoccupied lands"), which along with its various legal implications, has been argued in hundreds of court cases about land title over the years. In 2014, in *Tsilhqot'in Nation v. British Columbia*, the Supreme Court of Canada struck down *terra nullius* as a concept that applies to lands that Indigenous Peoples lived on and used before the arrival of Europeans. Further, in its 2015 final report, the Truth and Reconciliation Commission of Canada said: "We call upon all religious denominations and faith groups . . . to repudiate concepts used to justify European sovereignty over Indigenous lands and peoples, such as the Doctrine of Discovery and *terra nullius*."[24]

Eskimo: This term came into use in the seventeenth century to describe the Indigenous People who traditionally inhabit the Arctic regions in what are now Canada, Greenland, and Siberia. The term is rooted in explorer lexicon, and sometimes has inappropriate qualifiers depending on the explorer who claimed first contact—hence the so-called *Mackenzie Eskimos* in the Canadian Arctic.

The correct term—*Inuit*—began to emerge as a term in English in the early 1960s and became accepted English-language use, in line with what Inuit have always called themselves. The use of *Inuit* was one of the earliest examples of an Indigenous group in Canada changing terminology to assert their identity.

folklore: This term is commonly used in anthropology, archaeology, and art history to refer to the traditional cultural practices of Indigenous Peoples, the common people or "folk," and other predominantly non-Western groups. It also appears in the title of a UN agency: the World Intellectual Property Organization Intergovernmental Committee on Intellectual Property and Genetic Resources, Traditional Knowledge and Folklore—which is an example of how archaic terminology continues to persist. The term can be taken to imply that there is a differentiation and hierarchy between Indigenous Peoples' cultural practices and those of Western cultures, especially Western "high culture."

The problematic nature of the term makes it best to avoid: *cultural practice* is more appropriate.

heathen/pagan: These terms describe Indigenous Peoples as non-Christian or non-Hebrew with the connotation that their religions are therefore unenlightened and lacking in spiritual, cultural, and moral codes. They were originally applied to Indigenous Peoples by missionaries, so they also connote that Indigenous religions are morally corrupt. This connotation justified oppressive legislation in Canada, including the outlawing of the Potlatch among Indigenous Peoples of the West Coast and of the Sundance among Indigenous Peoples of the Prairies. The terms *heathen* and *pagan* have largely fallen out of use, but are common in missionary and explorer logs, and early Canadian government documents and legislation. If a current work quotes from these historical sources, it is important to establish that the terminology is no longer appropriate in, for example, a paragraph to introduce the content or in a footnote.

Indian: This term was commonly used to describe the hundreds of distinct nations of Indigenous Peoples throughout North, Central, and South America and the Caribbean. It traces back to the explorer tradition and was coined by Columbus as he was "looking for Asia. . . . [He was] going to find India. . . . And so [he] looked at the first peoples . . . on the shores and said, these must be Indians."[25] The term, therefore, was a misnomer from the start, although it was widely used by explorers and missionaries throughout the fifteenth, sixteenth, and seventeenth centuries, and was also commonly used in early anthropological texts, Canadian federal government documents, and Canadian and American mainstream society up to the present day.

Avoid this term as a general descriptor of identity. Use *First Nations* or *Indigenous Peoples* instead, with the clear understanding that *First Nations* describes Indigenous Peoples within Canada who do not identify as Métis or Inuit.

It is appropriate to use *Indian* to refer to the status of individual people under the Indian Act. In these situations, it is better to say *Status Indian*, or even *Status Indian under the Indian Act*, to clarify the specific context of use. Note that the Indian Act is a controversial piece of legislation, often under discussion among Indigenous Peoples. It may, therefore, undergo changes that will alter the context for terminology.

land claim: This term was originally used by Indigenous Peoples in the late 1960s to describe their right to ownership over, or compensation for, lands they traditionally occupied. Largely due to the increased recognition of Indigenous Peoples' title to Traditional Territories by the Supreme Court of British Columbia in the Calder case and the James Bay Project injunction, both in 1973, the Department of Indian Affairs and Northern Development (DIAND) adopted the term and applied it to its land claims policy in 1974. As the DIAND policy did not fully recognize Indigenous Title to land, the term gradually began to fall out of use among Indigenous Peoples, starting in the early 1980s, except when referring to the DIAND policy. The word *claim* in the term is problematic for Indigenous Peoples because it implies that they must apply to obtain ownership over land, not that they have inherent ownership. Due to the problematic nature of the term, *Indigenous Title* is more appropriate.

legends/mythology/myths/tales: These terms are often applied to Oral Traditions. This is offensive to Indigenous Peoples because the terms imply that Oral Traditions are insignificant, not based in reality, or not relevant. The term *legends* can also be construed this way, although *legends* can be acceptable to Indigenous Peoples in the sense that Oral Traditions describe past events that are legendary. To avoid misunderstanding, it's best to use terms such as *Oral Traditions* and *Traditional Stories*.

Native: This term was one of the most common descriptors of Indigenous Peoples in Canada, and other parts of the world, throughout the colonial period and into the 1980s. It has fallen out of use in Canada for the most part, but still has currency in the United States (i.e., the term *Native American*). The term is problematic because of possible confusion with its wider definition of a "local inhabitant or life form," and because it does not denote that there are many distinct Indigenous groups.

peace pipe: A made-up, erroneous "Indigenous object" or "Indigenous ceremony," which may or may not be about the authentic Indigenous practice of the Sacred Pipe (Ceremony).

prehistory: This term remains common in anthropological, historical, and art history texts. It implies that only written documents count as legitimate "history," and that Indigenous Peoples were not making and documenting history until they came into contact with Europeans. The term is erroneous and ethnocentric because it does not acknowledge Oral Traditions. The Supreme Court of Canada, however, does. In 1997, in *Delgamuukw v. British Columbia*, the court noted that "the laws of evidence must be adapted in order that [oral histories] can be accommodated and placed on an equal footing with the types of historical evidence that courts are familiar with."

primitive: This term was commonly used to describe Indigenous Peoples by explorers and missionaries throughout the fifteenth, sixteenth, and seventeenth centuries, and was also commonly used in anthropological texts and in early Canadian federal government documents and letters. The relevant OED definitions of *primitive* are "an original inhabitant, an aboriginal; a person belonging to a preliterate, nonindustrial society," and "that which recalls an early or ancient period; simple, unsophisticated or crude things or people as a class." The term gradually faded from common use, starting around the 1940s, and is now widely considered unacceptable. The term is considered degrading and inappropriate, as well as carrying evolutionary connotations.

rain/war dance: Made-up, erroneous terms for "Indigenous dances" supposedly done before going to war or to bring rain. These terms may or may not be referring to authentic Indigenous spiritual practices to show reverence for, and ask help from, the Creator.

Redman/Redskin: An offensive term for an individual Indigenous man or for Indigenous Peoples of the Western Hemisphere as a whole.

ritual/ritualistic: These terms were first used by missionaries in reference to Indigenous religious ceremonies, such as the Potlatch, the Sundance, and the Sweat Lodge. The terms imply that Indigenous religions are not legitimate religions, but rather more cult-like, thus implying an element of evil. The term is judgemental, Christiancentric, and inappropriate.

savage: This term was commonly used to describe Indigenous Peoples by explorers and missionaries throughout the fifteenth, sixteenth, and seventeenth centuries, and was also commonly used in early anthropological texts as late as the nineteenth century. The term also had currency in Canadian federal government documents and letters concerning "Indian affairs" up to the early twentieth century. The relevant OED definition for *savage* is "living in a wild state; belonging to a people regarded as primitive and uncivilized." Around the 1940s, the term began to gradually fade from common use and is now widely considered unacceptable. The term is clearly degrading and not appropriate to describe complex Indigenous societies that exist throughout the world. It also has evolutionary connotations.

self-government: This term was originally conceptualized and used by Indigenous Peoples in the late 1970s to describe their right to govern their own affairs. DIAND adopted the term and applied it to its community-based self-government policy in 1984. As the DIAND policy was more of a municipal government model and did not fully recognize governmental powers to the extent that most Indigenous Peoples were asserting, the term began to fall out of use among Indigenous Peoples starting in the late 1980s, except when referring to the DIAND policy. Due to the problematic nature of the term, *self-determination* is more appropriate. *Self-determination* is also the term used in UNDRIP.

squaw: An offensive term for an Indigenous woman.

tomahawk: An erroneous umbrella term for Indigenous axe-type weapons.

tom-tom: An erroneous term for an Indigenous drum, or a term describing a stereotyped drum beat.

tribe/tribal: This term has a somewhat ambiguous status among Indigenous Peoples in Canada.

As a general descriptor of Indigenous Peoples, it is problematic. Like *band, tribe* describes something looser than *nation, people,* or *society.* The relevant OED definition is "a particular race of recognized ancestry: a family." This alone makes *tribe* a less-than-accurate descriptor of Indigenous Peoples. *Tribe* also has older, more degrading meanings that cling to it. For example, the *Concise Oxford Dictionary of Current English, Sixth Edition,* published in 1998, defines *tribe* as "a group of primitive families under a recognized chief."

The term *tribe* (lowercase) is still used in certain instances, however, such as *tribal police,* to describe a reserve policing unit. In Canada, some Indigenous Peoples use *Tribe* (uppercase) as a way to refer to themselves, as in the Blood Tribe. These are acceptable uses.

It should also be noted that *tribe* still has currency in the United States among Indigenous Peoples.

uncivilized: This term traces back to explorer and missionary logs (and was later adopted by anthropology and Canadian government bureaucratic and legislative text). Like *barbarian,* it is evolutionary in nature and carries connotations of "violent unstructured peoples" with little or no social organization, who are far less refined than European-based societies, or even unrefined. In the missionary context, the term also carries a connotation of a people who are "un-Christian" and therefore backward, evil, and in need of conversion.

PRINCIPLE 11: INAPPROPRIATE TERMINOLOGY
Works should avoid inappropriate terminology used in reference to Indigenous Peoples, except when:
- specifically describing or discussing this terminology as terminology
- referring to a proper name, or the name of an institution or document, that contains the terminology
- quoting from a source that contains the terminology (e.g., a historical source)

If a work quotes from a historical source that uses inappropriate terminology, it is important to flag this content. This means discussing the terminology in a footnote or endnote, or, better yet, in a paragraph in run of text.

Appropriate terms

This section reviews a sampling of appropriate terminology as applied to Indigenous Peoples.

Indigenous Peoples have their own terms in their own languages for most of these terms (not for terms related to the collective rights of Indigenous Peoples, because these arose in legislative and legal contexts during the twentieth century). So, many of the words presented in this section are English translations. Translations came about partly because English has become the language spoken by the greatest number of Indigenous Peoples in Canada. The primacy of English among Indigenous Peoples comes from encroachment by Canada's dominant culture and from enforcement of the English language in the residential school system.

Many terms in this section are capitalized counter to the recommendations of conventional style guides. For a discussion of capitalization in Indigenous style, see chapter 7.

Aboriginal: This term gained currency in the 1990s as an appropriate way to refer to Indigenous Peoples in Canada. It is embedded in Section 35 of Canada's constitution and in Section 25 of the Charter of Rights and Freedoms (although lowercase there). It is also part of the language of many court cases and legal documents. The term's currency may stem from the Royal Commission on Aboriginal Peoples, which was established in 1992 and concluded in 1996, and which was key in setting a context for reconciliation in Canada.

Aboriginal is still an appropriate term, but is being replaced by *Indigenous*—a choice often made by Indigenous Peoples themselves—possibly in recognition of UNDRIP, which dates from 2007. The process has been gradual. For example, the final report of the Truth and Reconciliation Commission, completed in 2015, uses *Aboriginal* and *Indigenous* interchangeably. In other contexts, *Aboriginal* has been dropped. For example, the National Aboriginal Achievement Foundation changed its name to Indspire in 2012, and describes itself as an "Indigenous-led registered charity." CBC Aboriginal changed its name to CBC Indigenous in 2016.

Aboriginal is always an adjective, never a noun: an Aboriginal person, Aboriginal Peoples. For more details on how to use *Aboriginal*, see the entry for *Indigenous*. It follows the same rules.

the Creator: This term has become widely accepted by Indigenous Peoples to describe the supreme being who made the world and all life, placed peoples on specific territories, and gave them laws to live by. It is also the divine figure that is worshipped in various religions and ceremonies. The term has become the most widely accepted English term by Indigenous Peoples and is generally preferred over, and should replace, other terms such as *God* and *the Great Spirit*.

First Nations: This term was originally coined by Indigenous Peoples in the late 1970s, partly as an alternative to inappropriate terms such as *Native* and *Indian*, which were in common usage at the time. It was adopted by the national political organization, the Assembly of First Nations (previously the National Indian Brotherhood), in the early 1980s. In the 1990s, the term gradually became adopted by the general Canadian population.

The term has strong political connotations: it refers to separate nations that occupied territory before the arrival of Europeans. The term also has a double meaning in that it is sometimes used to describe a reserve or a group within a larger nation (e.g., the Westbank First Nation, which is actually a small portion of the Okanagan Nation).

First Nations refers to a segment of Indigenous Peoples in Canada. To use it in a context that describes all Indigenous Peoples in Canada, you need to say "First Nations, Inuit, and the Métis"; or, depending on your meaning (see the entries for *Inuit* and *Métis*), "First Nations, Inuit, and Métis peoples." In that context, critics of the term, such as Métis leader Howard Adams, have pointed out that the word *first* can be interpreted as elitist.

It is also worth noting that *First Nations* is not used in reference to Indigenous Peoples in the United States—in fact, it is sometimes used to distinguish between Indigenous Peoples on either side of the border. For example, a welcome at a powwow in the United States might go "Welcome to all the First Nations people here," which would mean "Welcome to all the Indigenous people from Canada here."

First Nations as an adjective is always plural:

- A *First Nations person* is an individual who comes from a First Nation. You can also say, "She is First Nations."
- *First Nations people* are people who come from First Nations, but whose particular First Nations are not at issue—as in the example of the welcome to an American powwow.

It can also be a noun, which can be plural or singular:

- For example, *the First Nations of the Prairies* are all of the First Nations that live on the Prairies.
- You can also talk about a First Nation in particular, such as Buffalo Point First Nation.

First Peoples: This term is rarely used by Indigenous Peoples to describe themselves, although it is also not considered particularly offensive or problematic. It recognizes that Indigenous Peoples are distinct groups, without the political connotations of the term *First Nations*. It is not widely used in the literature, and some organizations have stopped using it, such as the Canada Council for the Arts. Other organizations have not: the Canadian Museum of History—Canada's national museum of history and identity—uses it for one of its permanent exhibitions, the First Peoples Hall.

Indigenous: This term is gaining currency, replacing *Aboriginal* in many contexts (except, notably, Canada's constitution, where Section 35 affirms "the existing aboriginal and treaty rights of the aboriginal peoples of Canada," and the Charter of Rights and Freedoms where Section 25 talks about "aboriginal, treaty or other rights and freedoms that pertain to the aboriginal peoples of Canada"). It is used in the UN Declaration on the Rights of Indigenous Peoples, which has perhaps driven an increasing preference for *Indigenous*. The Canadian government department DIAND (Department of Indian and Northern Affairs) is currently Indigenous and Northern Affairs Canada.

The term *Indigenous Peoples* is used to refer to First Nations, Inuit, and Métis peoples in Canada collectively, and also to refer to Indigenous Peoples worldwide collectively. In some contexts, specific language adds useful clarity, as in *the Indigenous Peoples in what is now Canada* or *Indigenous Peoples around the world*.

Indigenous is always an adjective. In Canada, use of the term goes like this:

- An *Indigenous person* is an individual who identifies as First Nations, Inuit, or Métis.

- *Indigenous Peoples* are the distinct societies of First Nations, Inuit, and Métis peoples in Canada. This term recognizes the cultural integrity and diversity of Indigenous Peoples.

- An *Indigenous People* is a single one of the distinct societies of First Nations, Inuit, and Métis peoples in Canada. Inuit, for example, are an Indigenous People. So are the Nisga'a, the Siksika, and the Haudenosaunee.

- *Indigenous people* refers to people who identify as First Nations, Inuit, or Métis in a context where their specific identity is not at issue. In chapter 1, Wendy Whitebear uses the term in reference to anyone who identifies as Indigenous—a use I also occasionally need in this book. In chapter 3, Lee Maracle uses it as a way to note the tendency of mainstream society to think of Indigenous Peoples as "all the same."

Indigenous Right: This term describes an inherent and original right possessed collectively by Indigenous Peoples, and, in some cases, by individual Indigenous people. Some Indigenous Rights have legal recognition in Canada, and some do not. So, the term can assert a moral and ethical imperative.

For example, hunting and fishing is a collective Indigenous Right: Indigenous Peoples in Canada have this right. It is also an Indigenous Right of individual Indigenous hunters and fishers. This right has some recognition in law—for example, the Supreme Court decision *R. v. Powley* in 2003 recognized hunting and fishing as an "aboriginal right" within section 35 of the Constitution Act, 1982 that includes the Métis. Some jurisdictions, however—notably Alberta—contest the legal basis of Métis hunting and fishing.

Ownership and control of Indigenous cultural property is another example of an Indigenous Right, but a right only exercised collectively and without, so far, legal recognition in Canada.

Indigenous Title: This term refers to the Indigenous Right to collective ownership and jurisdiction over land and resources. Some Indigenous Peoples have successfully negotiated title to their Traditional Territories, but not all. So, like *Indigenous Right, Indigenous Title* can express a moral and ethical imperative.

For example, you can talk about the Indigenous Title of the Nisga'a, which was recognized in a land allocation under the treaty the Nisga'a concluded with British Columbia in 1998. You can also talk about the Indigenous Title of the Lubicon Lake Cree in Alberta, who have no treaty and who continue to assert sovereignty over their Traditional Territory. Indigenous Title also has currency in the context of the Numbered Treaties, concluded between First Nations in what is now western Canada and Canada's government in the late 1800s, as in "What terms did First Nations negotiate in exchange for ceding Indigenous Title, and how well has Canada met those terms?"

Inuit/Inuk: *Inuit* is the term for the Indigenous People who traditionally inhabit the Arctic regions of what is now Canada, Greenland, and Siberia.

Inuit can be an adjective, as in "an Inuit agreement" or "an Inuit musician."

Inuit is also a collective noun. It means *the people*, so it does not take an article or the qualifier *people*. For example, you can say "Inuit are traditional hunters of the whale." (The following are **incorrect**: "The Inuit are traditional hunters of the whale"; "The Inuit people are traditional hunters of the whale.")

Inuk is a singular noun for an individual. Examples of its correct use include the following: "This Inuk is a celebrated Inuit musician." (The following are **incorrect**: "The musician is an Inuk"; "He is an Inuk musician.")

Métis: This term has many contexts in Canada. People who self-identify as Métis do so for different reasons.

In one of its meanings, *Métis* describes an Indigenous People who emerged during the fur trade from the intermarriage of people of European descent and people of Indigenous descent. These people were at the centre of the Red River Resistance of 1869–70 and the Riel Resistance of 1885. The term *the Métis*—a collective noun with the definite article—can be taken to refer exclusively to this group (some commentators refer to them as "the historic Métis"). The Métis who lived at Red River at the time of the Red River Resistance were both French-speaking and English-speaking—a result of the involvement of France in the fur trade through Montréal, and of England in the fur trade through Hudson Bay. *Métis*, of course, is a French term that means "mixed." The English-speaking Métis at Red River sometimes referred to themselves as Half-breeds, which is a term that has fallen out of use, although it is not necessarily offensive.

In another of its meanings, *Metis*, without the accent, is a way English-speaking people of mixed Indigenous and non-Indigenous ancestry might refer to themselves, including those of Red River heritage and those of other heritages. Generally, *Métis*, with the accent in place, has currency as an umbrella term, even in contexts where other words from the French language are rendered without accents. For example, a 2017 article in the *Globe and Mail* used *Montreal* (no accent) and *Métis* (with the accent).

Métis also refers to people who identify as having mixed Indigenous and non-Indigenous heritage and who do not descend from the Métis of Red River. The term *Métis peoples* (lowercase and plural *peoples*) recognizes the complex of possible identities, and can be used as an unambiguous umbrella term to encompass everyone of mixed Indigenous and non-Indigenous heritage, including people of Red River heritage and others.

As a substitute for the term *Indigenous Peoples*, the phrase "First Nations, Inuit, and the Métis" could imply a focus on the Métis of Red River heritage in the final term. The phrase "First Nations, Inuit, and Métis peoples" indicates a broad focus on all people of mixed Indigenous and non-Indigenous heritage in the final term.

As a noun, *Métis* can be plural or singular: "He is Métis"; "Alberta is the only province in Canada that has designated land for the Métis."

Métis is also an adjective: Métis heritage, a Métis person.

Nation: This term has become widely accepted by Indigenous Peoples to describe separate Indigenous groups as political entities. It is an assertion that Indigenous Peoples meet the four criteria of nationhood under customary international law (as first set out in the Montevideo Convention of 1933), which are a permanent population, a definite occupied territory, a government, and the ability to enter into relations with other nations.

Nation is usually embedded in the name of a particular Indigenous People, and as such is capitalized—for example, Six Nations of the Grand River, the Métis Nation of Alberta, and Bigstone Cree Nation.

You might use *nation*, lowercase, where you wanted to emphasize the nationhood of Indigenous Peoples in a general context, as in "the nations of North America before contact with Europeans."

self-determination: In international law, this term is referred to as "The Divine Right of People," which was born out of the American (1776) and French (1789–99) revolutions. The term denotes the right of peoples to choose freely how they would be governed. This term has currency among Indigenous Peoples, replacing the term *self-government*. *Self-government* is still used in the specific context of discussing DIAND policies dating from the 1980s.

Status Indian: This term describes the status of individual people under the Indian Act. This is an appropriate term in this particular context and is accepted by Indigenous people as describing this context. Because of the problematic nature of *Indian* in general, however, it is best to clarify that you mean *Status Indian under the Indian Act.*

Note that the Indian Act is a controversial piece of legislation, often under discussion among Indigenous Peoples. It may, therefore, undergo changes that will alter the context for terminology.

Treaty Right: This term describes a right held by Indigenous Peoples collectively, and by individual Indigenous people, because of treaties Indigenous Peoples negotiated with Canada's government. Examples of Treaty Rights in Canada include provision of reserves, provision of education, and provision of health care (health care was originally negotiated under Treaty Six and later extended to all First Nations covered by treaty).

Names of particular Indigenous Peoples

Before the arrival of Europeans in North America, all Indigenous Peoples had names to identify themselves that, in most cases, were a variation of the words *the people* in their own language. During the colonial period in North America, English terms for Indigenous Peoples—coined in a variety of ways—emerged. Indigenous Peoples themselves maintained their own terminology, but the coined English terms became widespread in colonial society because Indigenous people often did not speak English and did not have access to colonial society.

Explorers, missionaries, and anthropologists coined most of these terms. The most common derivations included the following:

- a name associated with the first European to encounter an Indigenous group (e.g., Thompson Indians, Mackenzie Eskimos)
- an arbitrary English name based on some observation about an Indigenous group (e.g., Blackfoot, Flathead)

- an anglicized name based on a word heard in the language of an Indigenous group (e.g., Kwagiulth, Navajo, Salish, Nootka)
- an anglicized name based on a word for the group they heard in the language of another Indigenous People (e.g., Chipewyan, based on what they were called in Cree)
- a name based on a reasonable approximation of the word an Indigenous group used to identify themselves in their own language (e.g., Haida, Dene, Okanagan)

This last method, although the most appropriate, was also the most rare.

In the later colonial period in Canada, as generations of Indigenous children were introduced to English and systematically denied access to their languages through the residential school system, most Indigenous Peoples acquiesced to the terminology that had become established in English. This general trend, however, began to reverse in the early 1980s, when many Indigenous Peoples began to reestablish their original names.

This process has often involved awkward anglicizations, and the names of Indigenous Peoples in English often have several spellings. For example:

- The name *Ojibway* originates in the colonial period based on an anglicization of a word the Cree used to describe this Indigenous People. Although a single Indigenous People, groupings of this nation have separate names, such as "Chippewa" or "Assiniboine." In the 1980s, this Indigenous People began to assert their original name, which means *the people* in their language. Common spellings for the original name varied—for example, Nishnabwe, Anishnabay, Anishinabek, and Nishnawbay. In the 1990s, this Indigenous People generally agreed that the spelling Anishinaabe was a closer approximation of a phonetic English spelling. A variety of spellings remain in circulation, however, including Anishnaabe, Anishnawbe, Anishnabe, and Anishinaabeg.

- The Kwagiulth were termed *Kwakiutl* in the early 1800s by the anthropologist Franz Boas, who produced a vast body of literature about them. In the 1980s, this Indigenous People generally agreed that the spelling Kwagiulth is a closer approximation of a phonetic English spelling. More recently, Kwakwaka'wakw is gaining currency as the name for this Indigenous People, but the previous spellings also have currency. For example, the Kwakiutl District Council in Campbell River, BC, has nine member Nations.

The work of reestablishing and establishing the traditional names of Indigenous Nations (and appropriate spellings) is ongoing and being done by several institutions, including Indigenous institutions and Indigenous Nations. Here is a sampling of some other appropriate names:[26]

Carrier becomes:	**Dakelh**
Gitkasanin becomes:	**Gitxsan**
Iroquois becomes:	**Haudenosaunee**
Blood becomes:	**Kainai**
Mohawk becomes:	**Kanien'keha:ka**
Kootney becomes:	**Ktunaxa**
Micmac becomes:	**Mi'kmaq**
Assiniboine becomes:	**Nakoda**, or **Nakota**
Blackfoot becomes:	**Niisitapi**
Nishga or Nisga becomes:	**Nisga'a**
Thompson becomes:	**Nlaka'pamux**
Nootka becomes:	**Nuu'chah'nult**, or **Nuu'chah'nulth**
Bella Coola becomes:	**Nuxalk**
Peigan becomes:	**Piikuni**
Shuswap becomes:	**Secwepemc**
Lillooet becomes:	**Stl'atl'imx**
Okanagan becomes:	**Syilx**
Sarcee becomes:	**Tsuut'ina**, or **Tsuu T'ina**

There is no complete standard reference on correct names and spellings for all the Indigenous Peoples in Canada. As an editor or publisher trying to do the right thing in terms of accuracy, consistency, and showing respect on the page, you have two options.

First, you can ask the Indigenous Peoples at the centre of a work for the spelling of their names. This is the most respectful procedure, and is practical most of the time.

Second, you can choose to follow names and spellings compiled by others in consultation with Indigenous Peoples. In Canada, two current and useful compilations include the guide from the Canadian Association of University Teachers (CAUT) on acknowledging Traditional Territories and the list of First Nations in British Columbia developed by the X̱wi7x̱wa Library at the University of British Columbia. Other compilations—useful for the broader context of North America and as second references on Indigenous names in Canada—include Tribal Nations Maps and the website of the National Museum of the American Indian, Smithsonian Institution. (This book includes an appendix about these resources.)

Compilations such as these are evolving documents. As they are used—and considered and reconsidered by Indigenous scholars— they will no doubt undergo corrections and grow in detail. Make sure you have the most current version.

The method you choose to follow for Indigenous names in a work needs acknowledgement and explanation in the work. Perhaps, for example, you have consulted the Indigenous People at the centre of a work for their correct name and how to spell it; for Indigenous Peoples that the work names only in passing, you have followed the CAUT guide. It would be good to say this in an editor's introduction, for example, or in a note attached to the first instance of one of the names in the work.

PRINCIPLE 12: THE NAMES OF INDIGENOUS PEOPLES

Indigenous style uses the names for Indigenous Peoples that Indigenous Peoples use for themselves. It establishes these names through consultation with Indigenous Peoples, and compilations of names done through consultation with Indigenous Peoples.

Indigenous style provides notes of explanation about editorial decisions related to names. This is to acknowledge that Indigenous Peoples' names in English have evolved and are evolving.

Exceptions to this principle include:

- specifically describing or discussing another term that has been used as a name for an Indigenous People
- referring to a proper name, or the name of an institution or document, that contains another name
- quoting from a source that contains another name (e.g., a historical source)

7

Specific editorial issues

This chapter covers issues not yet discussed in this guide, and also restates some issues for ease of reference.

Academic freedom and Indigenous style

Collaboration is the key to working with Indigenous Peoples in a culturally appropriate way. Some academics, however, say that collaboration infringes academic freedom.

Here, for example, is what three Canadian political scientists say in an April 2017 article in the *International Indigenous Policy Journal*:

> In previous decades, . . . the majority of university-based professors designed, conducted, and published their studies on Indigenous Peoples with little regard to what participants and communities wanted. Researchers were encouraged to exercise their academic freedom to pursue research questions that interested them. . . . Scholars and scientists have slowly begun to recognize that in the past some of their studies had harmful effects on Indigenous communities and that new approaches were necessary for research involving Indigenous topics. . . . Consequently, there has been an increased demand for community-based research focusing on partnership and a corresponding decline in non-community-based approaches

> that emphasize the autonomy of researchers. An important
> consequence of these trends is a decline in the diversity of
> perspectives as researchers are putting aside their academic
> freedom to share authority over the research with participating
> communities. Our analysis suggests that . . . not all Indigenous-
> focused research should use a community-based research
> partnership model.[27]

The authors go on to argue that noncollaborative academic research and publication can still, and should, follow recognized ethical guidelines.

As someone working in Indigenous publishing, how should you approach works by non-Indigenous academics that conflict with the principle of Indigenous collaboration?

First, before you make a decision to publish or not publish a non-collaborative work, and with the consent of the author, open lines of communication to the Indigenous Peoples at the centre of the work. They may already be aware of the author and the work, and it's possible that they will see value in the work, despite not collaborating in it.

Second, ask the author to provide a commentary that might open the work and that speaks directly to its gaps in collaboration or its rationale for being noncollaborative. Ask whether the author might consider including a response to that discussion by the Indigenous Peoples at the centre of the work.

Third, if you are non-Indigenous, have an Indigenous editor evaluate the work and your editorial changes. Or, if you are Indigenous, get another Indigenous editor to give you a second opinion.

Finally, if you decide to publish, keep all lines of communication open at all times. *Your* process, as a publisher or editor of works by or about Indigenous Peoples, should aim for collaboration.

Biased language

Indigenous publishing requires an alert ear for how the attitudes of colonialism are embedded in word choices.

This section presents some common examples of subtle bias.

Indigenous agency

Colonial language communicates paternalism—the idea that Indigenous Peoples are not capable of thinking and acting for themselves.

Paternalism shows up in word choices like this: "The Numbered Treaties provided First Nations with reserves, education, and health care." The problem here is that First Nations sound like passive recipients of benefits, instead of active negotiators of Treaty Rights. Here are some better, more accurate wordings: "First Nations negotiated the Numbered Treaties with Canada's government to secure reserves, education, and health care for their people and future generations"; or "Through the negotiation of the Numbered Treaties with Canada's government, First Nations established their present-day and continuing Treaty Rights to reserves, education, and health care."

Another example: "The fur trade swept up Indigenous Peoples in a new economy based on supplying beaver pelts to French and English traders." This wording suggests Indigenous Peoples were *acted on*, instead of *acting*. A better, more accurate wording: "Indigenous Peoples engaged in the new economy of the fur trade, in which they supplied beaver pelts to French and English traders in exchange for European goods such as metal implements and guns."

Indigenous goals

Subtle bias shows up in word choices to describe the political goals of Indigenous Peoples. Consider the difference between *demanding* something and *asserting* something. You might use *demand* to describe a complaint or a whine: a child, for example, might demand dessert. You would use *assert* to describe a justified action: you *assert* authority, you *assert* rights.

In the context of Indigenous Title, *assert* is the appropriate word. The Nisga'a did not spend a century *demanding* Indigenous Title to their Traditional Territory (because this is an Indigenous Right they always had and still possess): they spent a century *asserting* Indigenous Title to their Traditional Territory.

Indigenous resilience

Pessimistic language is another form of subtle bias. For example, compare these statements: first, "Indigenous Peoples struggle with the legacy of the residential school system"; second, "Indigenous Peoples acknowledge the legacy of the residential school system, and the importance of appropriate compensation and apology from Canada's government in moving forward." The first statement makes Indigenous Peoples victims and casts doubt on their power to overcome trauma. The second statement recognizes their resilience, agency, and future.

Capitalization

Indigenous style uses capitals where conventional style does not. It is a deliberate decision that redresses mainstream society's history of regarding Indigenous Peoples as having no legitimate national identities; governmental, social, spiritual, or religious institutions; or collective rights.

This section presents a sample of terminology: not every term that should be capitalized appears here. When you come across a term that is not here, and you are wondering whether to capitalize it, look for a parallel example in this section. Also consider whether the term relates to Indigenous identity, institutions, or rights—in which case, capitalization is probably in order. If you're not sure, ask the Indigenous Peoples at the centre of the content how they view the term.

Capitalized terms for Indigenous identities

Chelsea Vowel says: "I always capitalize the various terms used to describe Indigenous peoples. This is deliberate; the terms are proper nouns and adjectives referring to specific groups. 'To captalize or not to capitalize' ends up being a heated debate at times, but I feel it is a measure of respect to always capitalize our names."[28]

For a discussion of the meaning and currency of the following terms, see chapter 6.

Aboriginal

The annual conference of Aboriginal educators took place in Vancouver.

First Nations

Northern Cree is a First Nations recording group that performed at the Grammy Awards in 2017.

Some First Nations in British Columbia have chosen to fight wildfires instead of evacuating their communities, noting that living in a fire zone "is not new to us."

First Peoples

European settlement in North America posed challenges for First Peoples.

Indigenous

The University of Toronto has more than four hundred Indigenous students.

Indigenous Peoples are diverse and culturally distinct.

Inuit/Inuk

Inuit are celebrating the creation of a marine protected area in Tallurutiup Imanga (Lancaster Sound), a successful conclusion to almost forty years of Inuit lobbying.

Atanarjuat: The Fast Runner, a 2001 film from Inuit director Zacharias Kunuk, presents the Traditional Story of the Inuk who battles an evil spirit disrupting his community.

Métis

The Métis have a long history in Canada, dating from the beginnings of the fur trade in the 1600s.

Canada's constitution recognizes Métis peoples among the Aboriginal peoples of Canada.

Survivor

The Truth and Reconciliation Commission documented testimonies from more than seven thousand residential school Survivors.

I am an Intergenerational Survivor.

Capitalized terms for Indigenous institutions
Chief

He is Chief of Driftpile Cree Nation.

Several Chiefs attended the First Ministers conference.

Clan; Clan System; Matriarch

The Haudenosaunee Confederacy has a total of nine Clans. Three Clans are common to all member nations, and five Clans are common to two or three member nations. A ninth Clan, the Eel Clan, is unique to the Onondaga.

The Clan System is a matrilineal social and political institution of the Haudenosaunee Confederacy.

She is Matriarch of the Bear Clan.

Creator; Creation

The meeting began with a prayer to the Creator.

People have a responsibility to care for Creation.

Elder

The students start every day by smudging, led by an Elder from the community.

Indigenous Voice

The Indigenous Voice is among the literatures of the world, and comes from Indigenous Peoples speaking for themselves, with connection to their past, present, and future, and in an evolving conversation with their Traditional Knowledge and Oral Traditions.

Longhouse

The Longhouse is a democratic institution based on consensus.

But: Many families lived together in longhouses, which were the living quarters of people of the same Clan.

Medicine Man; Medicine Woman

Medicine Men and Medicine Women have spiritual significance in Indigenous societies.

Midewiwin/Midewin

Like Christianity, Midewiwin is a religion.

Oral Tradition

The Oral Tradition of the Secwepemc includes a Traditional Story about the creation of salmon.

Respect for Oral Traditions includes following cultural Protocols about

Sacred Stories and seasonal stories, such as Winter Stories and Summer Stories.

Potlatch
Guests play an important role in the Potlatch as witnesses to gifts that acknowledge a family's inheritance.

The family held a Potlatch to honour the passing of the Elder.

But: The family potlatched to name their first son.

Protocols (cultural)
Indigenous Peoples have cultural Protocols about respecting Elders and Oral Traditions.

Sacred Pipe Ceremony; Pipe Carrier
During the Sacred Pipe Ceremony, the people pray not only for their own well-being, but for that of all human beings and the whole of Creation.

The Pipe Carrier, entrusted with the care of the Sacred Pipe on behalf of the people, brings the Sacred Pipe to the centre of the circle and unwraps it.

Seven Fires
The Oral Tradition of the Anishinaabe records the prophecy of the Seven Fires, which is also recorded in a Wampum Belt.

Sundance
No filming or photography is allowed during the Sundance, which is a sacred ceremony held during the summer.

Sweat Lodge
Amiskwaciy Academy invites Edmontonians to experience the spiritual, physical, and emotional cleansing of the Sweat Lodge as part of reconciliation.

Traditional Knowledge
The preferred method of harvesting wild rice by hand—by poling a canoe and knocking the rice—is part of the Traditional Knowledge of the Anishinaabe.

Vision Quest
The young man is going on a Vision Quest, where he will fast alone, and seek spiritual guidance and purpose.

Warrior Society
During the traditional hunts of the Plains Cree, the Warrior Society maintained discipline.

Wampum; Wampum Belt
In 1989, New York State returned twelve Wampum Belts to the Onondaga. Guswenta (Kaswentha), the Two Row Wampum, records a treaty that began in 1613 between the Haudenosaunee and European settlers.

Capitalized terms for Indigenous collective rights

Indigenous Land; Indigenous Title; Traditional Territory
Indigenous Peoples' assertion of Indigenous Title flows from their unbroken occupation and use of their Traditional Territories.
We celebrate the Indigenous Lands on which our city is located.

Indigenous Right
The inherent, collective right of Indigenous Peoples to speak their own languages and practise their own cultures is an Indigenous Right.

Status Indian
Filmmaker Howard Adler is a Status Indian under the Indian Act from Lac des Mille Lacs First Nation in Ontario.

Treaty Right
The First Nations who negotiated the Numbered Treaties with the Crown have education as a Treaty Right: it is not "free education," but rather education paid for in advance by the terms of the treaties.

PRINCIPLE 13: TERMS THAT SHOULD BE CAPITALIZED
Terms for Indigenous identities; Indigenous governmental, social, spiritual, and religious institutions; and Indigenous collective rights should be capitalized.

Indigenous colloquial English
As early as the late nineteenth century, so-called "Indian humorists" in the United States, such as Creek author Alexander Posey, began

writing in a form of Indigenous colloquial English, which was then referred to as *Este Charte*. An American writer of the time, Jace Weaver, made this observation about *Este Charte* and Creek writers: "To write or speak 'correctly broken English' is almost impossible for anyone who isn't born with it."[29] In the late 1960s, Indigenous academics coined the term *Red English* as they began to trace Indigenous colloquial English from its origins through to contemporary Creek authors such as Louis (Little Coon) Oliver and Joy Harjo.[30]

"Red English" is sometimes referred to as *Rez English* in Canada and is commonly used as a literary technique by high-profile Indigenous writers such as Jeannette Armstrong, Lee Maracle, Louise Halfe, and Maria Campbell. Jeannette Armstrong's Canadian bestselling novel *Slash*, for example, begins as follows: "School started that morning with old Horseface hollering at everybody to line up. Boy, it was cold. My ears hurting. I shoulda took my toque, I guess."[31]

Here's another example of Indigenous colloquial English from *Stories of the Road Allowance People* by renowned Métis author Maria Campbell:

> *Dah stories der not bad you know*
> *jus crazy*
> *Nobody knows for shore what hees true*
> *I don tink nobody he care eeder*
> *Dey jus tell dah stories cause Crow*
> *he makes damn good storytelling*
> *Some mans der like dat you know.*[32]

Stories of the Road Allowance People is one of the most unrestrained examples of Indigenous colloquial English published to date. In her introduction, Maria Campbell writes, "I am a young and inexperienced storyteller compared to the people who teach me. And although I speak my language I had to relearn it, to decolonize it, or at least begin the process of decolonization. . . . I give them (the stories) to you in the dialect and rhythm of my village and my father's generation."

In the foreword to *Stories of the Road Allowance People,* Ron Marken points out that academics such as J. A. Cuddon have missed the point of cultural colloquial English when making statements such as, "Poetry belonging to this tradition is composed orally. . . . As a rule it is a product of illiterate or semi-literate societies."[33] On the contrary, Marken argues, "The accents and grammar you will hear in this book are uncommon, but do not mistake them for unsophistication. . . . These stories and poems have come through a long journey to be with us from *Mitchif* through literal translations through the Queen's Imperial English and back to the earth in village English. . . . Our European concepts of 'voice' are hedged with assumptions and undermined with problems. Voice equals speech."[34]

Indigenous colloquial English, in its various forms, is a cultural expression of how Indigenous people speak informally and communicate within their communities. As such, it should receive the linguistic recognition and legitimacy afforded to forms of African American colloquial speech and to patois developed in the Caribbean and other parts of the world.

PRINCIPLE 14: INDIGENOUS COLLOQUIAL ENGLISH
Indigenous style recognizes Indigenous colloquial English as a legitimate literary device that should not be edited into "proper" English.

Indigenous cultural integrity

There are various ways in which Indigenous cultural integrity is not respected in the writing and publishing process. Among the most common are the following:

- Indigenous cultural materials are written down incorrectly or misinterpreted through European-based cultural perspectives.
- Indigenous cultural property is claimed by "authors" who are retelling or transcribing Traditional Knowledge or Oral Traditions.

- Indigenous cultural property that attaches to particular Elders, families, or Clans is appropriated (i.e., told without permission or claimed by authors).

- Indigenous cultural property that has specific Protocols associated with its use—for example, stories that can only be told by certain people, in certain ceremonies, or at certain times of the year—are published in transgression of Protocols.

- Indigenous cultural property that is sacred and not intended for the public domain—including some stories, ceremonies, dances, and objects such as masks—is appropriated and presented in books.

The risk of these transgressions is highest in works by non-Indigenous authors, or by Indigenous authors writing about Indigenous Peoples outside their own heritage.

To avoid these transgressions, you need to get to know your authors. A context of trust is key—trust that your authors, as people of integrity, have followed Protocols and established consent among the members of an Indigenous People to use their cultural property.

As a publisher or editor, you should also consider ways to acknowledge and benefit the true authors of Indigenous cultural property. Chapter 3 discusses ways of doing this, including assigning copyright to the Indigenous People who own the cultural property; negotiating royalty and licensing agreements with the Indigenous People for using it; and wording attributions to show that the "conventional author" is really someone who has transcribed or recorded Indigenous cultural property, not someone who has "written it."

Indigenous trauma and the publishing process

A recent phenomenon in Canadian publishing is what could be called "Indigenous trauma titles." These include residential school narratives and narratives of other colonial oppression. The following titles have all far exceeded the sales requirements for Canadian best-seller status in the last five years: *They Called Me Number One* by Bev Sellars (Talon

Books, 2012); *Clearing the Plains* by James Daschuk (University of Regina Press, 2013); *The Education of Augie Merasty* by Joseph Augie Merasty (University of Regina Press, 2015); and *I Am Not a Number* by Jenny Dupuis and Kathy Kacer (Second Story Press, 2016).

This trend is set to continue, with the public's growing attention to the Sixties Scoop, and to murdered and missing Indigenous women and girls.

Indigenous trauma is an area where Indigenous editors have particular importance. Indigenous editors often come from backgrounds that include these difficult and complex issues, which helps them navigate the intense collaboration—including, at times, collaboration with Elders, communities, and families—that these titles require.

Editing and publishing Indigenous trauma takes extreme sensitivity, and must be guided by the principle of "do no more harm." It also takes time. Editors have to get to know authors, and seek to understand the motivations of authors in sharing their stories. These motivations can include healing, retribution, anger, sorrow, exposing perpetrators (or colonization in general), and contributing to reconciliation. Authors may have a combination of motivations. Understanding an author's motivations—and taking the time to do that properly—helps clarify the process needed to write, edit, and publish the story, and reach the best possible outcome.

PRINCIPLE 15: EDITING AND PUBLISHING INDIGENOUS TRAUMA

Editing and publishing Indigenous trauma requires extreme sensitivity, and is best engaged through the skills of Indigenous editors. It involves the principle of "do no more harm." It also involves taking time with authors, and, as needed, with family, community, and Elders.

Indigenous words in the English language

Conventional style guides recommend italicizing words and phrases in languages other than English, except in cases where the word or phrase is commonly understood. One rule of thumb is that if the word or phrase appears in the English dictionary you are using, then it should be set in roman. For example, the term *café au lait* (from French, with the accent) and *barista* (from Italian) appear in several English dictionaries, so you would not italicize them: "The barista takes the customer's order for café au lait."

Many words of Indigenous origin appear in several English dictionaries. Here, for example, are words listed in the free online dictionaries of Collins, Merriam-Webster, and Oxford:·

canoe
hammock
igloo
kayak
maize
moccasin
moose
muskeg
pemmican
potato
raccoon
saskatoon: Collins and Merriam-Webster list this term, which refers to the plant and berry. Oxford lists only the city (Saskatoon) in its free online resource, although the term for the plant and berry appears in the longer, etymological *Oxford English Dictionary*.
skunk
sockeye (salmon)
squash (the vegetable)
tamarack
tipi: Collins and Merriam-Webster list *tepee* as an alternate spelling; Oxford lists *tepee* as the preferred spelling, and *tipi* and *teepee* as alternate spellings.
toboggan
tomato
wapiti

So, none of these words would appear in italics by conventional style.

I regret that English has swallowed these words. These words bear witness to the history of Indigenous Peoples in contact with Europeans. They often represent technologies and foods that Indigenous Peoples introduced to Europeans. Their presentation as "English" terms fails to acknowledge the contributions Indigenous Peoples have made to mainstream culture and the English language, and fails to educate readers who may not be aware of these contributions.

A key goal of Indigenous style is to show respect on the page. Indigenous style could recommend italicizing these words to emphasize their foreign origin in Indigenous languages. I think, though, that this would be a clunky solution. For one thing, these are Indigenous words rendered for the English ear. If you italicize *saskatoon*, what would you do with *misâskwatômin*, which is the actual Cree word of origin? It seems to me that italics is best reserved for *misâskwatômin*.

Another solution is to include notes about words of Indigenous origin in an etymological glossary in the back matter of a work. The etymology of Indigenous-origin words can be complicated. Of the online dictionaries, for example, Collins and Oxford (not Merriam-Webster) supply notes on Indigenous etymology, but sometimes disagree on the source language. For *muskeg*, Collins lists the derivation as Algonquian or Cree; Oxford lists it as Cree only. Spellings from the source language also differ: Collins and Oxford agree that *raccoon* comes from Algonquian, but Collins renders the source word as *ärähkun* and Oxford renders it *aroughcun*. So, include a discussion about how you arrived at the etymological information in the glossary. Consider consulting several etymological sources, and summarizing points of agreement and disagreement. Consider consulting people fluent in the Indigenous language at issue for their insights, especially for words derived from the language of the Indigenous Peoples at the centre of the work.

Consider, also, using the word the Indigenous People use for their own language. Generally, this is not the word with currency in English. For example, the language of the Syilx is Nsyilxcn.

Indigenous-derived place names

I also recommend including place names in a glossary of Indigenous-origin words. List place names that a work mentions, and also names not mentioned but associated with the language of the Indigenous Peoples at the centre of the work.

Here are some examples of place names with Cree origins:

Amisk: from *amisk*, which means "beaver"

Athabasca: from the Cree "*Y* dialect" word *ayapaskaah*, meaning "place of rolling terrain" (or "uneven terrain")

(Fort) **Chipewyan:** from *ociipweyen*, meaning "pointed skins," which refers to how the Dene Peoples prepared hides

Manitoba: from *manitou*, meaning "the Creator"

Namao: from *namew*, meaning "sturgeon"

Saskatchewan: from *kisiskaaciiwan*, meaning "swift or fast current"

Wabamun (Lake): from *waapamon*, meaning "mirror" or "reflection"

Wabasca (River): from *waapaskah*, meaning "white terrain" (or "light-coloured terrain")

Wapasu (Creek): from *waapaasiw*, meaning "whitish" or "light coloured" usually in reference to hair or fur

Wetaskiwin: from *wehtaskiiwan*, meaning "place of peace"

Other place names derived from Indigenous languages include Deseronto, Chilliwack, Lillooet, Mississauga, Restigouche, Shawinigan, and Témiscaming.[35]

PRINCIPLE 16: ENGLISH WORDS OF INDIGENOUS ORIGIN
Indigenous style acknowledges words of Indigenous origin, including place names, to show respect for the contribution of Indigenous Peoples to the English language and mainstream culture. The recommended acknowledgement is an etymological glossary of Indigenous-origin English words. The glossary should include words specifically used in a work and words related to the language of the Indigenous Peoples at the centre of a work.

Metis-specific editing issues

Red River Resistance of 1869–70, Riel Resistance of 1885

The term *rebellion* does not describe the events that took place in Red River in 1869–70 or in Batoche in 1885, though it remains a common descriptor for them in content about the history of Canada and Louis Riel. OED defines *rebellion* as "an organized armed resistance to an established ruler or government." The mismatch between this definition and the events of Red River and Batoche lies in the words *established ruler or government*. In 1869–70, Canada had no jurisdiction in Red River (the Hudson's Bay Company did). By 1885, Canada had claimed what is now Saskatchewan and Alberta, but had not established any governing structures, and especially had not negotiated with the Peoples who were already there governing themselves: the Métis and the Cree, in particular. The term *rebellion* also involves open conflict—which did take place, but was not the goal in either case. In Red River and in Batoche, the Métis goal was negotiation. The Métis petitioned the Canadian government to recognize their title to the lands they occupied, instead of opening their lands to settlement. The term *resistance*, as opposed to *rebellion*, also allows for the idea of *opposition to an invading force*, which captures the situation of the Métis and Cree at Red River and at Batoche more accurately.

PRINCIPLE 17: THE MÉTIS RESISTANCES
The appropriate terms for the events in the history of the Métis and Canada in 1869–70 and 1885 are the *Red River Resistance* and the *Riel Resistance*.

Road Allowance People
Road Allowance People refers to a chapter in the history and identity of the Métis after they moved west following the Red River Resistance and the Riel Resistance. It is appropriate to use the term in this context.

The Red River Resistance was successful in the sense that it negotiated the creation of Manitoba as a province that joined Confederation with language rights for French-speaking peoples. The rest of the west (except what became the province of British Columbia) "joined" Canada in a land transfer from the Hudson's Bay Company, which had "owned" Rupert's Land as a colonial fur-trading entity.

The Red River Resistance was not successful, though, in its aim of establishing a land base for the Métis. Instead of directly conferring land, Canada's government allotted 140,000 acres to the heads of Métis families under the scrip system. The system was flawed: it worked to dispossess families of their land, because the stipulations for exchanging scrip for land were not achievable for most Métis. Speculators bought the scrip and took the land.

The Métis settlement at Batoche came about as the Métis left Red River looking to maintain their way of life in lands further west under less settlement pressure. After the Riel Resistance of 1885 at Batoche, they moved west again.

The Road Allowance People were essentially small Métis communities situated on the Crown land that existed in the easements between roads. The Métis lived there because racism and discrimination prevented them from living in settler towns. Because they lived on Crown land, they did not pay taxes and their children were not allowed to attend school. As settler towns grew, the Road Allowance People often found themselves evicted from their homes, again.

Pan-Indigenous terms

This guide uses a pan-Indigenous term, *Indigenous Peoples*, because it is talking about issues in publishing and editing that cut across all Indigenous identities.

In general, however, it is best to avoid blanket terms.

For example, it is not appropriate to say "Theresa Cardinal is an Indigenous person." A better wording is "Theresa Cardinal is Cree from Saddle Lake Cree Nation." Names are part of the way we render identity. Use the words that individual people use for themselves, and, if you don't know what words to use, ask.

Here's another example. It is not appropriate for a work about Winnipeg to refer generally to "First Nations and their Traditional Territories" in an acknowledgement (especially since this wording would exclude the Métis). It should name the particular Indigenous Peoples. In the context of Winnipeg, the guide from the Canadian Association of University Teachers (CAUT) on acknowledging Traditional Territories mentions specifically the Anishinaabeg, Cree, Oji-Cree, Dakota, Dene, and the Métis Nation.

Precision is important. It shows respect by acknowledging the diversity and distinctness of Indigenous Peoples.

Possessives that offend

It is a common error to use possessives to describe Indigenous Peoples, as in "Canada's Indigenous Peoples," or "our Aboriginal Peoples," or "the First Peoples of Canada." These possessives imply that Indigenous Peoples are "owned" by Euro-colonial states.

Indigenous Peoples assert sovereignty and many do not identify as Canadian.

To describe Indigenous Peoples as located in Canada, appropriate wordings include "Indigenous Peoples in Canada" or "Indigenous Peoples in what is now Canada."

PRINCIPLE 18: INAPPROPRIATE POSSESSIVES
Indigenous Peoples are independent sovereign nations that predate Euro-colonial states and are not "owned" by Euro-colonial states. Indigenous style therefore avoids the use of possessives that imply this, such as "Canada's Indigenous Peoples," "our Indigenous Peoples," and "the Indigenous Peoples of Canada."

Reusing already-published material

Indigenous cultural material

Beware of repeating past errors. Indigenous content published in the past, or contained in archives, may not have followed the Protocols of the source Indigenous People. This content includes, in particular, information from Traditional Knowledge and Oral Traditions, and photographs of ceremonies and cultural objects.

To reuse this material in a publication, you need to be sure you have the permission of the Indigenous People it comes from. Permission involves either the trust you place in the author, or (in cases of non-Indigenous authors, or Indigenous authors writing outside their own context) by checking with Elders of the Indigenous People who own the material as their cultural property.

In some cases, you may not be able to establish the Indigenous People who own a cultural property, because the photographer or transcriber did not record the source or recorded it inaccurately. Avoid using this material: you cannot establish its significance and, if you need permission, you do not have it.

PRINCIPLE 19: REUSING CULTURAL MATERIAL IN ARCHIVES OR ALREADY IN PUBLICATION

Indigenous style recognizes that materials contained in archives, or already published in works about Indigenous Peoples, may have violated cultural Protocols. Authors, editors, and publishers need to establish permission to use these materials from the Indigenous Peoples who own them as their cultural property, before these materials appear in new works by or about Indigenous Peoples.

Historical translations

Consider this passage:

> In the coming of the Long Knives, with their firewater and quick-shooting guns, we are weak and our people have been woefully

slain and impoverished. You say this will be stopped. We are glad to have it stopped. What you tell us about this strong power which will govern with good law and treat the Indian the same as the white man, makes us glad. My brother, I believe you and I am thankful.

This is a translation of the words of Issapoomahksika (Crowfoot), spoken in 1874, concerning the intention of the RCMP to regulate trading at Fort Whoop-Up, near present-day Lethbridge in what is now Alberta. Three works that use this passage report the audience as either the Methodist missionary John McDougall or RCMP Colonel James Macleod.[36]

Issapoomahksika was speaking in the language of the Siksika. None of the works indicate who was translating, but each reports the words exactly the same way, so perhaps the words accurately capture what the translator said. But I believe they do not accurately capture, in English, what Issapoomahksika said in his own language. *Long Knives* refers to the non-Indigenous traders at Fort Whoop-Up, *firewater* refers to alcohol, *quick-shooting guns* refers to repeating rifles, *strong power* refers to the British Crown, and *Indian* refers to Indigenous Peoples. So why not say, in republishing these words, *traders, alcohol, repeating rifles, the British Crown*, and *Indigenous Peoples*? A parallel example would be to translate a passage from French about puzzles (*casse-têtes*) using the literal term *head-breakers*.

Republishing the "historical" translation of Issapoomahksika words, and republishing other translations like it, perpetuates colonial stereotypes of Indigenous Peoples as unsophisticated.

PRINCIPLE 20: HISTORICAL TRANSLATIONS
Update historical translations from Indigenous languages to avoid literal renditions of terms.

Stereotypes and assumptions

Stereotypes and assumptions relay unexamined generalizations. They are a disservice to the people they claim to describe and a disservice to readers.

Stereotypes and assumptions in a work signal the need for substantial editing. At best, they rest on the surface, as tangents that the author can delete or rewrite. At worst, they go to the core of a work as starting points or key ideas.

In reworking stereotypes and assumptions, specificity is your friend. Who exactly is the author talking about? Who exactly has the author been talking to? Breaking down generalizations starts with these questions, and may lead to solutions as simple as stating the answers to these questions. The solutions, however, may also lie in resetting a work through proper collaboration with the Indigenous Peoples at its centre.

This section presents some common stereotypes and assumptions about Indigenous Peoples in Canada.

All Indigenous people live in harmony with nature. Content about projects with environmental impacts—such as pipelines, oil sands development, and industrial forestry—and content about climate change risk stating this stereotype. It is true that particular Indigenous Peoples oppose particular projects, and true that some speak out on climate change. It is also true that the Traditional Knowledge and Oral Traditions of many Indigenous Peoples express particular kinds of connectedness between humans and the natural world. Stick to those truths by being specific about who is expressing opposition or speaking out, what project or issue they are addressing, and what aspects of their Traditional Knowledge and Oral Traditions inform their perspective.

All Indigenous people live on reserves. Watch for this stereotype in content about, for example, schools and living conditions on reserves. The quality of on-reserve education, housing, health care, and water is fundamentally important, but it is also important to recognize that reserves account for only a segment of the Indigenous population in Canada.

Reserve mostly applies to First Nations people who are Status Indians under the Indian Act. So, generally, it does not apply to Métis peoples, Inuit, or people who identify as First Nations but are not Status Indians. (Alberta has eight Métis Settlements that loosely fit the idea of reserves. Unlike reserves, however, they have no connection to Canada's federal government.) In addition, less than half of Status Indians (44%) who could live on reserves do live on reserves, according to Canada's 2016 census, and the off-reserve population is growing more quickly (at 49% per year) than the on-reserve population (at 13% per year). Statistics Canada identifies Winnipeg, Edmonton, Vancouver, and Toronto as the urban centres with the largest populations of off-reserve Status Indians.

The stereotype that all Indigenous people live on reserves has a counterpart: that Indigenous people who live off-reserve do not have specific Indigenous identities. In content about Indigenous people who live in urban areas, watch for statements that describe individuals with blanket monikers such as "First Nations people" or "Indigenous people." The best wordings describe the particular identities of individuals with the words they use to describe themselves.

Indigenous Peoples migrated to North America. The Oral Traditions of Indigenous Peoples in North America indicate that Indigenous Peoples have lived for millennia in the places they live, although some record ancient migrations *within* the Americas (not *to* the Americas). This needs saying in content discussing migration theories. Indigenous style means Indigenous Peoples *speaking*: the relationship of Indigenous Peoples to their Traditional Territories, stretching back to time immemorial, is part of what they say.

Traditional Knowledge and creative license

Indigenous authors have "Indigenous National Artistic License," which means they have permission to innovate Traditional Knowledge if they are in a position of trust with the Indigenous People to whom they belong.

A position of trust means: 1) the Indigenous author is a stakeholder with a custodial relationship to the Traditional Knowledge; and 2) the Indigenous author has a relationship to, and responsibility for, the Nation the Traditional Knowledge derives from, and the Indigenous Protocols associated with it. With these relationships intact, an ethical use of Traditional Knowledge is able to result.

This does not mean that only Indigenous Peoples can use Traditional Knowledge. A non-Indigenous author is also able to enter into a relationship with an Indigenous Nation and access Traditional Knowledge for a certain use. These authors need to secure prior informed consent and mutually agreed terms with the source Indigenous Nation. Non-Indigenous authors do not have Indigenous National Artistic License.

Translating Indigenous works

Indigenous language translation is emerging as an important element of the Indigenous cultural renaissance. It is also an important aspect of reconciliation and of recovering from the damage caused by residential schools. Indigenous publishers are well positioned to publish in Indigenous languages, which should be part of their mandate and publishing program. Non-Indigenous publishers should seek out Indigenous editors to assist in the process of translation and in gaining access to Indigenous language translators.

Many Indigenous language translators argue that, because of the complexity of Indigenous languages, they should be paid more than, for example, English-French translators. Proper acknowledgement is also important: Indigenous language translators deserve high respect, given their key role in Indigenous language revitalization.

If an Indigenous Traditional Story is "translated back" into an Indigenous language for publication, it is essential to use the language of the story's source Indigenous Nation.

In the context of other works, the language of the Indigenous author is the most appropriate choice for translation (unless the market for the work is a particular Indigenous language group).

PRINCIPLE 21: INDIGENOUS LANGUAGE TRANSLATION

Indigenous style recognizes that Indigenous language translation is an important part of Indigenous Peoples' cultural reclamation and resurgence.

- Proper acknowledgement of, and compensation for, translators is essential, as a sign of respect for their role in Indigenous language revitalization.
- Translations of Traditional Stories should use the language of the source Indigenous Nation.
- Translations of other works should use the Indigenous language of the author, unless there is a good reason not to.

Verb tense

Avoid the common error of describing Indigenous Peoples in the past tense, as in "they held Potlatches" or "they told Sacred Stories passed down through Oral Traditions" or "they had Traditional Territories where they hunted and fished."

They *hold* Potlatches, they *tell* Sacred Stories, they *have* Traditional Territories.

Referring to Indigenous Peoples in the past tense engages the following inappropriate, often offensive assumptions:

- that Indigenous Peoples no longer exist as distinct cultures
- that they no longer practise their cultural traditions
- that contemporary Indigenous Peoples have been assimilated into mainstream Canadian society to the point that they no longer identify with their ancestors, or that Indigenous cultures have been fundamentally altered or undermined through colonization

Indigenous Peoples have *not* been assimilated into mainstream Canadian society, despite over a century of legislation and official policy to force assimilation. Indigenous national and cultural paradigms have *not* been fundamentally altered or undermined through colonization. Indigenous Peoples are distinct and diverse, and going through processes of healing and reclamation. They are living cultures that adopt new technologies and adapt to new circumstances in a process of complex navigation, but not of acquiescence.

PRINCIPLE 22: THE PAST TENSE

Avoid the past tense in writing about Indigenous Peoples, except when:

- referring to an activity or event that specifically and exclusively took place in the past
- referring to an Indigenous cultural activity that is no longer practised (as this is rarely the case, seek confirmation with an authoritative member of the particular Indigenous People)
- using a quotation that uses the past tense

APPENDIX A

Summary of Indigenous style principles

PRINCIPLE 1: THE PURPOSE OF INDIGENOUS STYLE
The purpose of Indigenous style is to produce works that:
- reflect Indigenous realities as they are perceived by Indigenous Peoples
- are truthful and insightful in their Indigenous content
- are respectful of the cultural integrity of Indigenous Peoples

PRINCIPLE 2: WHEN INDIGENOUS STYLE AND CONVENTIONAL STYLES DISAGREE
Works by Indigenous authors or with Indigenous content should follow standard style references and house styles, except where these disagree with Indigenous style.

In these works, Indigenous style overrules other styles in cases of disagreement.

PRINCIPLE 3: INDIGENOUS LITERATURES AND CANLIT
Indigenous Literatures are their own canon and not a subgroup of CanLit. Contemporary Indigenous authors' works are an extension of Traditional Knowledge systems, Indigenous histories, histories of colonization, and contemporary realities. Indigenous Literatures frame

these experiences for Indigenous readers and provide non-Indigenous readers with context for these realities.

Contemporary Indigenous Literatures connect to and extend Traditional Stories and Oral Traditions that have existed for centuries and millennia, and that long predate CanLit.

PRINCIPLE 4: RECOGNIZING INDIGENOUS IDENTITY

Indigenous style recognizes that Indigenous Peoples view themselves according to the following key principles:

- They are diverse, distinct cultures.
- They exist as part of an ongoing continuum through the generations tracing back to their ancient ancestors.
- They have not been assimilated into mainstream Canadian society, and their national and cultural paradigms have not been fundamentally altered or undermined through colonization.
- They are currently in a process of cultural reclamation and rejuvenation, marked by significant participation from Indigenous youth.
- Natural cultural change and adaptation do not mean that Indigenous Peoples have acquiesced to mainstream Canadian society, nor that Indigenous cultures have been fundamentally altered or undermined.

PRINCIPLE 5: INDIGENOUS CULTURAL PROPERTY

Indigenous style involves publishing practices that recognize and respect Indigenous cultural property.

PRINCIPLE 6: COLLABORATION

Work in collaboration with Indigenous Peoples and authors to ensure that Indigenous material is expressed with the highest possible level of cultural authenticity, and in a manner that follows Indigenous Protocols and maintains Indigenous cultural integrity.

PRINCIPLE 7: ELDERS

Indigenous style recognizes the significance of Elders in the cultural integrity of Indigenous Peoples and as authentic sources of Indigenous cultural information.

Indigenous style follows Protocols to observe respect for Elders.

PRINCIPLE 8. WORKING WITH TRADITIONAL KNOWLEDGE AND ORAL TRADITIONS

Indigenous style recognizes Traditional Knowledge and Oral Traditions as Indigenous cultural property, owned by Indigenous Peoples and over which Indigenous Peoples exert control. This recognition has bearing on permission and copyright, and applies even when non-Indigenous laws do not require it.

Writers, editors, and publishers should make every effort to ensure that Indigenous Protocols are followed in the publication of Traditional Knowledge and Oral Traditions. Where culturally sensitive Indigenous materials are in question, writers, editors, and publishers should make every effort to consult an authoritative member of the particular Indigenous People for confirmation.

PRINCIPLE 9: THE ROLE OF RELATIONSHIP AND TRUST

Indigenous style recognizes the essential role of relationship and trust in producing works with authentic Indigenous content, and the source of relationship and trust in truthfulness, honesty, mindfulness about community impacts, and continuity with history and heritage.

PRINCIPLE 10: COMPENSATION

Indigenous style recognizes the importance of royalties to Indigenous Peoples and authors, and compensation to individual Indigenous contributors, as part of fair and respectful publishing relationships.

PRINCIPLE 11: INAPPROPRIATE TERMINOLOGY

Works should avoid inappropriate terminology used in reference to Indigenous Peoples, except when:

- specifically describing or discussing this terminology as terminology
- referring to a proper name, or the name of an institution or document, that contains the terminology
- quoting from a source that contains the terminology (e.g., a historical source)

If a work quotes from a historical source that uses inappropriate terminology, it is important to flag this content. This means discussing the terminology in a footnote or endnote, or, better yet, in a paragraph in run of text.

PRINCIPLE 12: THE NAMES OF INDIGENOUS PEOPLES

Indigenous style uses the names for Indigenous Peoples that Indigenous Peoples use for themselves. It establishes these names through consultation with Indigenous Peoples, and compilations of names done through consultation with Indigenous Peoples.

Indigenous style provides notes of explanation about editorial decisions related to names. This is to acknowledge that Indigenous Peoples' names in English have evolved and are evolving.

Exceptions to this principle include:

- specifically describing or discussing another term that has been used as a name for an Indigenous People
- referring to a proper name, or the name of an institution or document, that contains another name
- quoting from a source that contains another name (e.g., a historical source)

PRINCIPLE 13: TERMS THAT SHOULD BE CAPITALIZED

Terms for Indigenous identities; Indigenous governmental, social, spiritual, and religious institutions; and Indigenous collective rights should be capitalized.

PRINCIPLE 14: INDIGENOUS COLLOQUIAL ENGLISH

Indigenous style recognizes Indigenous colloquial English as a legitimate literary device that should not be edited into "proper" English.

PRINCIPLE 15: EDITING AND PUBLISHING INDIGENOUS TRAUMA

Editing and publishing Indigenous trauma requires extreme sensitivity, and is best engaged through the skills of Indigenous editors. It involves the principle of "do no more harm." It also involves taking time with authors, and, as needed, with family, community, and Elders.

PRINCIPLE 16: ENGLISH WORDS OF INDIGENOUS ORIGIN

Indigenous style acknowledges words of Indigenous origin, including place names, to show respect for the contribution of Indigenous Peoples to the English language and mainstream culture. The recommended acknowledgement is an etymological glossary of Indigenous-origin English words. The glossary should include words specifically used in a work and words related to the language of the Indigenous Peoples at the centre of a work.

PRINCIPLE 17: THE MÉTIS RESISTANCES

The appropriate terms for the events in the history of the Métis and Canada in 1869–70 and 1885 are the *Red River Resistance* and the *Riel Resistance*.

PRINCIPLE 18: INAPPROPRIATE POSSESSIVES

Indigenous Peoples are independent sovereign nations that predate Euro-colonial states and are not "owned" by Euro-colonial states. Indigenous style therefore avoids the use of possessives that imply this, such as "Canada's Indigenous Peoples," "our Indigenous Peoples," and "the Indigenous Peoples of Canada."

PRINCIPLE 19: REUSING CULTURAL MATERIAL IN ARCHIVES OR ALREADY IN PUBLICATION

Indigenous style recognizes that materials contained in archives, or already published in works about Indigenous Peoples, may have violated cultural Protocols. Authors, editors, and publishers need to establish permission to use these materials from the Indigenous Peoples who own them as their cultural property, before these materials appear in new works by or about Indigenous Peoples.

PRINCIPLE 20: HISTORICAL TRANSLATIONS

Update historical translations from Indigenous languages to avoid literal renditions of terms.

PRINCIPLE 21: INDIGENOUS LANGUAGE TRANSLATION

Indigenous style recognizes that Indigenous language translation is an important part of Indigenous Peoples' cultural reclamation and resurgence.

- Proper acknowledgement of, and compensation for, translators is essential as a sign of respect for their role in Indigenous language revitalization.

- Translations of Traditional Stories should use the language of the source Indigenous Nation.
- Translations of other works should use the Indigenous language of the author, unless there is a good reason not to.

PRINCIPLE 22: THE PAST TENSE

Avoid the past tense in writing about Indigenous Peoples, except when:

- referring to an activity or event that specifically and exclusively took place in the past
- referring to an Indigenous cultural activity that is no longer practised (as this is rarely the case, seek confirmation with an authoritative member of the particular Indigenous People)
- using a quotation that uses the past tense

APPENDIX B

Draft principles of the
Indigenous Editors Circle

These principles come from the Indigenous Editors Circle convened in Saskatoon in June 2015. In 2017, the Indigenous Editors Circle became a program at Humber College, Toronto.

The Indigenous Editors Circle promotes the following principles to support and develop Indigenous authors and editors in Canada.

1. Respectful representation of Indigenous Peoples in published books is a right protected by Section 35 of Canada's Constitution Act, 1982, and by Article 31 of the United Nations Declaration on the Rights of Indigenous Peoples.
2. Literatures by Indigenous authors and about Indigenous Peoples ought to be edited by Indigenous editors.
3. Ethical principles about Indigenous cultural heritage ownership ought to supercede copyright laws.
4. Indigenous communities have collective ownership over their Traditional Knowledge.
5. The publication of a book is all about clearly defined, transparent, respectful relationships.
6. Indigenous authors are not necessarily bound by the conventions of established literary genres.

7. It is the responsibility of the editor and therefore the publisher to mentor emerging Indigenous writers where possible.

8. Ceremony is a potential resource for building collaborative relationships built on sacred trust.

9. Vetting, reviewing, and consultation regarding Indigenous content needs to be by an Indigenous person.

10. Publishing houses need to take an interest in, and safeguard and support, the cultural integrity of Indigenous editors.

11. Any textbook containing Indigenous content currently used in a Canadian school must be approved by the Indigenous Editors Association.

12. Teams of reviewers and vetters must include culturally competent members.

The Indigenous Editors Circle recommends setting aside a specific portion of public funding for writers to support Indigenous writers.

The Indigenous Editors Circle envisions Canadian publishers that will:

1. respond responsibly to feedback about publications that are offensive to Indigenous readers;

2. undergo Indigenous cultural sensitivity training;

3. recruit and retain Indigenous editors to publish and develop Indigenous authors;

4. provide career guidance to new Indigenous authors, mindful of the potential responsibilities of authors to provide public readings in home communities that might be far away; and

5. respect the localities and diversities of place, language, sexual orientation, and multiple genders.

APPENDIX C

Compilations of names of Indigenous Peoples

These are four resources that compile the names of Indigenous Peoples in consultation with Indigenous Peoples. They are available online, and best used online because the resources are updated to reflect evolving spellings.

GUIDE TO ACKNOWLEDGING FIRST PEOPLES & TRADITIONAL TERRITORY, PUBLISHED BY THE CANADIAN ASSOCIATION OF UNIVERSITY TEACHERS (CAUT)

The best way to find this publication is to search its title, together with the term *CAUT*, on your web browser. You can also find the publication with the search function on the CAUT website.

LIST OF NAMES FOR INDIGENOUS PEOPLES IN BRITISH COLUMBIA, AVAILABLE FROM THE X̱WI7X̱WA LIBRARY, UNIVERSITY OF BRITISH COLUMBIA

On the X̱wi7x̱wa Library website, find the link *Collections*, and click on its sublink *Indigenous Knowledge Organization*. Click the link *X̱wi7x̱wa classification system* under the title "Classification System." Click the link *First Nations Names Authority List*.

TRIBAL NATIONS MAPS

This site offers maps for purchase that show the Traditional Territories of Indigenous Peoples with the names that Indigenous Peoples use for themselves. With your web browser, search *Tribal Nations Maps*.

THE NATIONAL MUSEUM OF THE AMERICAN INDIAN, SMITHSONIAN INSTITUTION

The museum lists more current, together with less current, names for Indigenous Peoples by region. On the museum website, click the *Explore* link, then *Collections*, then *Search Online Collections*, then *Peoples/Cultures*.

APPENDIX D

Gnaritas Nullius (No One's Knowledge): The Essence of Traditional Knowledge and Its Colonization through Western Legal Regimes*

*This paper first appeared in *Free Knowledge: Confronting the Commodification of Human Discovery*, edited by Patricia W. Elliott and Daryl H. Hepting (University of Regina Press, 2015). It has been edited to follow *Elements of Indigenous Style*. Republished with permission.

GREGORY YOUNGING

Despite centuries of oppression, Indigenous knowledge is rich, varied, and continues to evolve.

Prior to contact with Western peoples between three hundred to six hundred years ago, Indigenous Nations had developed and evolved knowledge systems that flourished for millennia over most of the earth's land mass. These knowledge systems are integrated with the ecosystems in Indigenous territories, and are rich and varied, ranging from soil and plant taxonomy, cultural and genetic information, animal husbandry, medicine and pharmacology, ecology, zoology, music, arts, architecture, social welfare, governance, conflict management, and many others.[1] This chapter will begin by briefly outlining a small sampling of the manifestations of Indigenous knowledge systems that existed before European contact and colonization, most of which continue to exist and evolve.

Significant Contributions to Humanity: Devalued and Diminished

In the northern part of the continent of South America, Indigenous Nations had charted the constellations, developed astrological charts, and constructed elaborate pyramids that parallel the pyramids in Egypt. In the mountains near the mid-west coast of the continent were complex city structures containing shaped stone buildings, stairs, walkways, and irrigation systems that still stand today. The ruins show precision-crafted buildings with neat regular lines, bevelled edges, and mortarless seams that characterize the best of Inca architecture.[2] In the interior of North America, Indigenous Nations constructed gigantic mounds, some in the shape of animal and human figures that can only be identified from an aerial view. Entombed bodies and metal tools have been found inside these mounds, indicating "a complex and advanced civilization at work."[3] Along the northwest coast of the continent, intricate wood longhouses were constructed, comprising village structures that continue to intrigue architects. The three hundred or so Indigenous Nations that lived in North America when Christopher Columbus arrived built their homes and arranged their settlements according to similar patterns and principles passed from generation to generation.[4]

Far beyond architecture, Indigenous design in North America had produced products including a variety of canoe designs, the kayak, snowshoes, sunglasses, and a multitude of farming and hunting implements. Gardening using hydroponics and advanced farming techniques were developed and practised on different continents by Indigenous Peoples producing a range of crops including corn, squash, beans, tomatoes, wheat, potatoes, and varieties of fruits. Throughout the Amazon basin, Indigenous farmers had overcome problems with termites and other insects by using extracts from trees that act as natural repellents—which Western scientists now struggle to understand and reproduce. Throughout North and South America, Indigenous farmers had a profound understanding of genetics, enabling them to experiment with new strains of potatoes. In the Andean region, Indigenous farmers knew that by taking pollen from one variety of corn and fertilizing the silk of another variety, they could create a corn with combined characteristics of the two parent crops.[5]

Major advances in the realm of health and herbal medicines had been developed throughout the continents of the Indigenous world. Shamans and traditional healers practised spiritual, herbal, and psychological techniques, including the placebo effect. Indigenous herbal specialists around the world gathered plants and studied and developed natural medicines that continue to surpass by far the advances in herbal medicine by non-Indigenous peoples. Indigenous knowledge systems have also made many significant contributions to the arts and humanities of the world. The technique of acid etching of designs of the Hohokam people in what is now southwestern Arizona (dating back to 500 BCE) predates the technique in Europe by three hundred years.[6] Stories of ancient times before human beings, stories of the creation of Indigenous Peoples, and other stories of spiritual, mythological, and legendary figures are rooted in the Oral Traditions of Indigenous Nations that have been passed down through generations and continue to fascinate many of the peoples of the world. Elaborate Indigenous artistic techniques and designs in sculpture, painting, music, drama, and dance continue to thrive in traditional and evolved forms, and have intrigued art historians and the art world for centuries.

In the area of governance, complex political systems exist among Indigenous Nations and include Chieftainships, Monarchies, and evidence of universal rights and democracy before any such concepts in Europe. The Haudenausaunee People of the Longhouse practise a democratic form of government and formed the League of the Six Nations Confederacy that would later influence the development of American and European democracy. Oral Traditions among the People of the Longhouse place the origin of the league at about 900 BCE,[7] although the Six Nations Confederacy was not officially formed until the early fifteenth century. Other United Nations structures along the northwest coast, eastern seaboard, and southern and northeast plains of North America developed between 2,500 and 1,500 years ago and far predate any such structures in Europe. Treaties and other economic, military, and political alliances between Indigenous Nations would continue through conflicts in the colonization process up to the present.

Indigenous knowledge systems represent the accumulated experience, wisdom, and know-how unique to nations, societies, and/or communities of people living in specific environments of America, Africa, Asia, and Oceania. These knowledge systems represent the accumulated knowledge of what was over 70 per cent of the earth's land mass before the era of colonization in the past few centuries—some ten thousand distinct Peoples and cultures. In the past, Eurocentric knowledge has condescendingly associated Indigenous knowledge with the primitive, the wild, and the natural.[8] This is the prevailing negative Eurocentric perception of Traditional Knowledge (TK) that forms the basis for the status quo. Despite the advances made by knowledge systems throughout the Indigenous world, the Western world's general response throughout the colonial and most of the post-colonial periods was to dismiss the value of TK. Since only European people could progress, all Indigenous knowledge was viewed as static and historical.[9]

Not all TK originates from Indigenous Peoples. Other forms of knowledge such as ancient Chinese medicine, Caribbean steel drum making and music, ancient Belgian weaving and lace-making techniques, and ancient Swiss yodelling have been considered to be forms of Traditional Knowledge. It is the case, however, that well over 95 percent of TK is derived from Indigenous Peoples. The term "Traditional Knowledge" differs from the term "Indigenous knowledge" in that it does not include contemporary Indigenous knowledge and knowledge developed from a combination of traditional and contemporary knowledge. The two terms are, however, sometimes used interchangeably. Certain voices in the discourse prefer the term Indigenous knowledge because TK can be interpreted as implying that Indigenous knowledge is static and does not evolve and adapt.[10] However, Traditional Knowledge is the term used in most national discourses and virtually all the international forums. Indigenous knowledge is not only "technical" but also empirical in nature. Its recipients' integrative insights, wisdom, ideas, perceptions, and innovative capabilities pertain to ecological, biological, geographical, and other physical phenomena. It has the capacity for total systems understanding and management.[11]

The World Intellectual Property Organization Inter-Governmental Committee on Intellectual Property, Traditional Knowledge, Genetic Resources and Folklore (WIPO IGC) was established by the World Intellectual Property Organization (WIPO) General Assembly in October 2000 as a United Nations international forum for debate and dialogue concerning the interplay between intellectual property and TK. In carrying out its ongoing mandate to establish international standards for the protection and regulation of the use of TK, WIPO developed the following definition of Traditional Knowledge for the purposes of a 1998–1999 fact-finding mission that led to the establishment of the IGC (that has come to be regarded somewhat as a standard definition):

Traditional knowledge refer[s] to tradition-based literary, artistic or scientific works; performances; inventions; scientific discoveries; designs; marks, names and symbols; undisclosed information; and all other tradition-based innovations and creations resulting from intellectual activity in the industrial, scientific, literary or artistic fields. "Tradition-based" refers to knowledge systems, creations, innovations and cultural expressions which have generally been transmitted from generation to generation; are generally regarded as pertaining to a particular people or its territory; and, are constantly evolving in response to a changing environment. Categories of traditional knowledge could include: agricultural knowledge; scientific knowledge; technical knowledge; ecological knowledge; medicinal knowledge, including related medicines and remedies; biodiversity-related knowledge; traditional cultural expressions ("expressions of folklore") in the form of music, dance, song, handicrafts, designs, stories and artwork; elements of language, such as names, geographical indications and symbols; and, movable cultural properties. Excluded from this description would be items not resulting from intellectual activity in the industrial, scientific, literary or artistic fields, such as human remains, languages in general, and other similar elements of "heritage" in the broad sense.[12]

Empirical-Like Knowledge as an Indigenous Methodology

Most of Western-based research has been conducted through the scientific process that has, in turn, produced most Western-based knowledge. Vine Deloria Jr. has characterized the effect of the scientific process as follows: "Eventually, we are told, the results of this research with many other reports, are digested by intellects of the highest order and the paradigm of scientific explanation moves steadily forward, reducing the number of secrets Mother Nature has left."[13] In contrast to Western-based scientific research methodology, there are emerging principles of Indigenous-based research that draw on Indigenous traditional methods of learning through lived experience including ecological and social interaction. Aspects of such methodologies can also be viewed in parallel with Western-based theories of: 1) historical methodology, regarding primary sources and oral tradition; and 2) discourse analysis, as expounded by Vivien Burr[14] and Kenneth Gergen.[15]

The historical method comprises the techniques and guidelines by which historians use primary sources and other evidence to research and then write history. The question of the nature, and indeed the possibility, of sound historical method is raised in the philosophy of history as a question of epistemology.[16] Aspects of the historical method and Indigenous epistemology also converge in the use of oral tradition, whereby the oral transmission of information from person to person is considered a legitimate method of knowledge acquisition. Whereas oral testimony derived from a person who was present at (or otherwise involved with) a past event can legitimately inform present and future generations of history, oral transmission of cultural knowledge flowing from the past legitimately informs Indigenous heritage in proceeding generations. In both cases, a form of exclusive expertise is extended to the person with empirical knowledge of the event, or the Elder with empirical and transgenerational cultural knowledge. In many cases, the historical method's oral tradition and Indigenous Oral Traditions are often the most reliable methods of knowledge acquisition, and, indeed, sometimes the best or only options.

With regard to discourse analysis, Burr and Gergen contended that "[o]ur ways of understanding the world are created and maintained by social processes."[17] Discourse is a form of social action that plays a part in producing the social world—including knowledge. Knowledge is created through social interaction in which we construct common truths and compete about what is true or false.[18] Although some understandings of TK can fit discourse analysis, more useful aspects are based fundamentally on Indigenous traditional methodologies that are now emerging as being useful to Indigenous research in contemporary contexts. Indigenous pedagogy paradigms are heavily based on the natural world and apprenticed relationships with Elders and other authoritative experts within Indigenous cultural confines. Within traditional Indigenous cultures, authority and respect are attributed to *Elders*—people who have acquired wisdom through life experiences, education (a process of gaining skills, knowledge, and understanding), and reflection.[19]

Perhaps the single most important precept of the Indigenous world view is the notion that the world is alive, conscious, and flowing with knowledge and energy. In his paper, "An Organic Arising: An Interpretation of Tikanga Based upon Maori Creation Traditions," Charles Royal states the following:

> *The natural world is not so much the repository of wisdom but rather is wisdom itself, flowing with purpose and design. We can say that the natural world is a mind to which all minds find their origin, their teacher and proper model. Indigenous knowledge is the fruit of this cosmic stream, arising organically when the world itself breathes through and inspires human cultural manifestation ... Leading from this view of the world being alive, conscious and wisdom filled is the obvious conclusion that all that we need to know, all that there is to know and all that we should know already exists in the world, daily birthed in the great cycle of life. That is, human cultural production is a natural organic expression arising from the contours, shapes and colours of the environments in which we dwell.[20]*

To carry this Indigenous principle into the contemporary context, it must be acknowledged that many Indigenous Peoples no longer dwell solely in what was "the world" to their ancestors (e.g., the natural world). Many Indigenous Peoples are now located in a world that consists of a complex physical and cultural layering of principles derived from nature and modernity. However, as emerging Indigenous research methodologies express, this does not mean that traditional models are not applicable and adaptable. Therefore, in contemporary research, Indigenous models can be adapted in the following ways: 1) interaction with the contemporary environment and the subsequent gained experience can be an important and relevant way of acquiring knowledge; and 2) authoritative figures who have accumulated a wealth of experience over time on particular aspects of the contemporary world can be afforded an Elder-like status for the purposes of research.

This Indigenous model of learning through experiencing is articulated further in Linda Tuhiwai Smith's *Decolonizing Methodologies: Research and Indigenous Peoples* as "intervening" and "connecting." Smith contends that, "[i]ntervening takes action research to mean literally the process of being pro-active and becoming involved as an interested worker for change." Intervening and getting involved in a process occurring in the world is therefore a legitimate method of acquiring knowledge through the benefit of an insider perspective to the process, while also engaging and affecting the process. With regard to connecting, Smith states, "[c]onnectedness positions individuals in sets of relationships with other people and with the environment."[21]

Sources of Indigenous Knowledge

Some key sources of Indigenous knowledge include:

1. learning from observation of cyclical patterns in ecosystems and other natural law;
2. learning from animals;
3. spiritual knowledge acquired through ceremonies;
4. learning through teachings in Indigenous stories and philosophies;
5. trial and error;
6. Indigenous empirical-like knowledge;
7. Oral Traditions;
8. learning from Elders' interpretations and intuition;
9. ancient ancestral knowledge;
10. learning through Indigenous theories and methodologies;
11. learning through unique aspects of the contemporary Indigenous condition.

However, these high-capacity, time-tested Indigenous knowledge systems have been devalued and diminished by having Eurocentric perceptions and institutions imposed upon them. In the process, many of the systems have been debased through misrepresentation, misappropriation, unauthorized use, and the separating of the content from its accompanying regulatory regime.

CUSTOMARY LAWS: DEVELOPED LEGAL REGIMES DEVALUED AND DIMINISHED

Indigenous Peoples have numerous internal Customary Laws associated with the use of Traditional Knowledge. These Customary Laws have also been called "Protocols" and are part of the laws that Indigenous Nations have been governed by for millennia and are primarily contained in Oral Traditions. Although, in lieu of the increased outside interest in TK and problems with interaction between TK and intellectual property rights (IPR) systems, there is a current movement among many Indigenous Nations to document their laws around the usage of their knowledge in written and/or digital format. In addition, many Indigenous Nations are developing methodologies for adapting and evolving Customary Laws so they will be effective in present-day situations.

Customary laws around the use of Traditional Knowledge vary greatly between Indigenous Nations.

Certain plant harvesting, songs, dances, stories, and dramatic performances can only be performed/recited and are owned by certain individuals, families, or clan members in certain settings and/or certain seasons and/or for certain Indigenous internal cultural reasons.

Crests, motifs, designs, and symbols, as well as herbal and medicinal techniques, are owned by certain individuals, families, or Clan members.

Artistic aspects of Traditional Knowledge, such as songs, dances, stories, dramatic performances, and herbal and medicinal techniques can only be shared in certain settings or spiritual ceremonies with individuals who have earned, inherited, and/or gone through a cultural and/or educational process.

Art forms and techniques, and herbal and medicinal techniques cannot be practised, and/or certain motifs cannot be used until the emerging trainee has apprenticed under a master of the technique.

Certain ceremonial art and herbal and medicinal techniques can only be shared for specific internal Indigenous cultural and/or spiritual reasons and within specific Indigenous cultural contexts.

These are but a few general examples of Customary Laws that Indigenous Nations around the world have developed over thousands years to regulate the use of Traditional Knowledge. Indigenous Customary Laws are intimately intertwined and connected with TK and form what can be viewed as whole and complete, integrated, complex Indigenous knowledge systems throughout the world. For example, speaking about Clan ownership in Nlaka'pamux Customary Law, Shirley Sterling states: "This concept of ownership by clans, nations and family groups and individuals of stories and other knowledge must be respected. The protocols for the use of collective knowledge from each cultural area and each First Nation would have to be identified and followed."[22]

Indigenous Customary Law, like other sources of law, is dynamic by its very nature. Like its subject matter—culture, practices, and traditions—it is not frozen in time. It has evolved with the social development of Indigenous Peoples. Indigenous Customary Law also has an inextricable communal nature. The social structures that recreate, exercise, and transmit this law through generations, and the protocols that govern these processes, are deeply rooted in the Traditional Territories of Indigenous Peoples, and, understandably, are inalienable from the land and environment itself.[23] Indigenous Customary Law is inseparable from Indigenous knowledge. In some Indigenous Nations, the abstract subtlety of Indigenous Customary Law is indivisible from cultural expressions such as stories, designs, and songs. That is, a story may have an underlying principle of environmental law or natural resource planning.[24] A song may explain the custodial relationship that a certain community has with a particular animal species. A design may be a symbol that expresses sovereignty over a territory, as well as the social hierarchy of a Nation's Clan System. A watchman's pole may be considered an assertion of Indigenous Title, tell a story of a historical figure, and have a sacred significance.[25]

Neither the common law nor international treaties place Indigenous Customary Law on equal footing with other sources of law. As a result, Traditional Knowledge is particularly vulnerable to continued misuse and appropriation without substantive legal protection. Indigenous Jurisprudence and Law should protect Indigenous knowledge. In relation to Eurocentric law, Indigenous Jurisprudence of each heritage should be seen as an issue of conflict of laws and comparative jurisprudence. With regard to its authority over Indigenous knowledge, Indigenous Law and Protocols should prevail over Eurocentric patent, trademark, or copyright laws.[26] However, due to a series of historical realities that will be considered below, the status quo is that Indigenous knowledge has become subjugated under European legal regimes, and intellectual property rights and other Eurocentric legal regimes trump or fail to recognize Indigenous Law. This has created a situation where TK is taken out of its Indigenous context and placed in Western contexts without the accompanying Indigenous Law, thus leaving TK vulnerable and often devoid of, or lacking in, its integrity.

European Systems: Intellectual Property Rights

One of the greatest ironies of the status quo in the interface between European and Indigenous knowledge management systems is that Indigenous systems predate European systems by centuries. This point can be highlighted by the historical reality that when Christopher Columbus landed in the Americas, hundreds of integrated knowledge systems, complete with regulatory regimes, had been functioning on the continent for generations, while no such regulatory regimes were in existence in Europe. What would now be termed "piracy," "unauthorized disclosure," and "copyright infringement" was common practice in sixteenth-century Europe. In the period of time leading up to the mid-sixteenth century, European authors' works were produced and sold without permission,[27] and inventors began to boycott the trade fair circuit based around Frankfurt because they would commonly have their ideas misappropriated. This section will briefly outline the development of some of the important milestones in Europe that led to the concept of "intellectual property" and the development of what became the intellectual property rights (IPR) system.

Copyright

The word "copyright" came into being as a reference to the sole right of the Stationers' Company to copy texts, first enacted in the second half of the sixteenth century in England. The Stationers' Company was a London-based booksellers' cartel that enjoyed a legislative monopoly over the trade in books in exchange for assistance in the suppression of "seditious" and "blasphemous" texts. An idea akin to the modern notion of copyright was developed in fifteenth-century Venice, predating the Industrial Revolution when creations were imbued with unprecedented social and economic value. The first such legislative award was made in 1486 to historian Marc Antonio Sabellico. The grant of copyright protection by Venetian authorities was meant to compensate inventors and stimulate invention. In 1545, the Venetian Council of Ten demanded that booksellers secure written proof that their publications had received authorial consent.[28]

Copyright as we know it began in 1710 with the enactment in England of the Statute of Anne. Prior to this, publishing was regulated by means of the Licensing Act, which required that all books be registered with the Stationers' Company. Thus, copyright was not introduced to deal with concerns of authors but to regulate the trade in books and to assuage the concerns of the booksellers and printers. The mention of the rights of authors in the preamble had more to do with window dressing than substantive protection. The preamble stated:

Whereas Printers, Booksellers and other persons have lately frequently taken the Liberty of printing, Reprinting and Publishing or causing to be Printed, Reprinted and Published Books and other writings without the consent of Authors or Proprietors of such Books and Writings to their very great Detriment, and too often to the ruin of them and their families.[29]

With the Statute of Anne came a time limit on the rights of authors: twenty-one years for the books already on the Stationers' register, and up to twenty-eight years for new books. It also introduced the concept of the public domain, a commons that encompasses documents and material of all kinds no longer protected by copyright. Regardless of ownership, once the term of copyright expires, intellectual property becomes the property of everyone. The physical embodiment of it may continue to belong to individuals or institutions, but the intellectual property falls into the public domain. However, if a new work is created that incorporates a work that is in the public domain, the new work is protected.

The enactment of this statute meant that two authorities governing the rights of authors existed in England: common law (the law created by decisions of judges), and statute law (the law created by legislation). The decisive case came in 1769 with the judgment in *Millar v. Taylor*. Millar was a London-based bookseller who brought the suit for copyright infringement against Taylor, a rival bookman who had published "The Seasons," a poem Millar "owned." Millar grounded his case in common law, arguing that he had purchased the rights to the poem in perpetuity. Taylor based his defence on the Statute of Anne, claiming that Millar's copyright had run its course and the poem was in the public domain.

The judge decided in favour of common law and Millar stated: "It is just, that an author should reap the pecuniary profit of his own ingenuity and labour. It is just, that another should not use his name without his consent. It is just that he should judge when to publish, or whether he will publish. It is fit he should not only chose the time, but the manner of publication, how many, what volume, what print. It is fit, he should choose to whose care he will trust the accuracy and correctness of the impression."[30] The Millar decision in favour of authorial rights stood for only five years. It was overturned in 1774 in the case of *Donaldson v. Beckett* (Donaldson being a pirate publisher, and Becket being an author) that established the notion of the balance of interests between creators and users in copyright.

Droit moral and droit d'auteur

Moral rights came into being in France in the eighteenth century. The moral rights theory holds that a creator is a sovereign individual and therefore his/her work is sovereign, and as such, must be respected. In Article 27, the United Nations Declaration of Human Rights states, "Everyone has the right to the production of moral and material interests resulting from scientific, literary or artistic production of which he is the author." This is balanced by article 2(1), which states that "[e]veryone has the right to freely participate in the cultural life of the community to enjoy the arts and to share in its benefits."[31] The Berne Convention for the Protection of Literary and Artistic Works of 1886 was the first international agreement on copyright in Europe. The convention enacted a moral rights clause at its Rome Congress in 1928. Article 6 of the convention states: "Independently of the author's economic rights, and even after the transfer of said rights, the author shall have the right to claim authorship of the work and to object to any distortion, mutilation or other modification of, or other derogatory action in relation to, the said work which would be prejudicial to his honour or reputation."[32] The concept of *droit moral* (moral rights) was introduced, which in turn led to the concept *droit d'auteur* (author's rights). *Droit moral* theory holds that the author/creator is sovereign, and therefore his/her work is sovereign and must be respected as such. *Droit d'auteur* holds that the rights of the author/creator are natural and inalienable rights and that the author/creator must be identified with, and credited for, the work.

Originality

The key criterion for copyright protection is that the work be "original." Originality does not mean that a work must be unique, one of a kind, and unlike anything else but rather that it be an original expression of the author, and not a copy of another work. The explanation of one American jurist, Judge Learned Hand, in 1936, is often quoted as a definition: "Borrowed work must not be for the plagiarist who is not himself *pro tano* an 'author'; but if by some magic a man who has never known it were to compose a new Keats 'Ode on a Grecian Urn,' he would be an 'author,' and, if he copyrighted it, others might not copy that poem, though they might of course copy Keats's."[33]

Ownership

Copyright in a work belongs in the first instance to the creator. Subsequently, it may be licensed or assigned, for example, to producers, publishers, and distributors who manufacture and market the work. If a work is produced during the course of employment as part of the employee's duties, however, the law stipulates that the rights are the employer's. Similarly, if a photograph, portrait, engraving, or print is commissioned, the person ordering the work and paying for it is deemed to own the copyright, unless there is an agreement to the contrary. There are thus two kinds of copyright owners operating in the cultural sector: corporations or businesses, and individual creators. In some countries, to have copyright protection, a work must be registered. In Canada, when someone creates a work, it is automatically protected under the Copyright Act, so long as the creator is Canadian or is resident here, or in a country that is a signatory to the international conventions, such as the Berne Convention, to which Canada belongs.

The so-called Anglo-American copyright systems (in Canada and the United States, and influencing and being adopted in other countries) have a primarily utilitarian logic. In return for enriching the public, creators are allowed to reap some of the fruits of their creative labours. But the monopoly thereby granted by the state is temporary, and the law expresses an interest in protecting the public's right to copyright material in the long term through the concept of the public domain. Hence, copyright's concern with "balance." In public policy terms, this can be understood as the tension between individual rights and public freedoms—that is, between the property rights of individuals and the right of society to its cultural heritage and to the freedom of information.

The continental system is based on the concept of the *droit d'auteur* as the "natural and inalienable" right of individual creators. The interests of creators are paramount, not those of the public, and moral rights are central. Moreover, these are deemed to be human rights, attached to the individual creator. They indicate that besides being a product, service, or a performance, a creation is connected to the person of its creator. Behind the painting, the text, or the film, lies the reputation of its author.[34]

Patents and Trademarks

The regulation of patents protecting industrial inventions, the oldest form of intellectual property, goes back to the Venetian Decree of 1474.[35] The concept of patents did not get widespread recognition in Europe with the passage of England's 1624 Statute of Monopolies. The Statute of Monopolies spoke of granting patents for "any manner of new manufactures." The Paris Convention for the Protection of Industrial Property was passed in 1883. The European Patent Convention was passed in 1973. Patents are granted to inventors to protect their inventions from being copied or used by others for a fixed time period, usually between seventeen and twenty years. Most industrialized countries now have a patent office to administer the application and regulation of patents. The main criteria for the granting of patents are that the invention must be "new, useful and unobvious ideas with practical application." This can include "new machines, products, processes, or improvements on existing technology."[36]

As European societies became increasingly industrialized, it became apparent that patents and copyright were not sufficient to protect all forms of intellectual property. In the eighteenth century, European countries in the process of industrialization developed the concept of "trademark," which was later legislated in the form of national trademark acts. Patent and trademark, along with copyright, now make up the current IPR system. Trademarks are used to support a company's claim that its products are unique as compared to similar products from other companies. The main criteria for granting trademarks are that the product is "authentic" and "useful." Most industrialized governments now have agencies to grant and administer trademarks. Once a trademark is applied for in its country of "origin," the trademark applicant can apply to have it registered in other countries to which it may wish to export its products. Some groupings of countries have multilateral trademark agreements, such as the Madrid Agreement Concerning the International Registration of Trademarks, which enables an applicant to be granted trademark in the thirty signatory countries with a single application.

Ratification by Canada of the latest versions of the Paris Convention (1967) and Berne Convention (1971) requires Canada to bring its intellectual property laws in line with the conventions. In the Irwin Essentials in Canadian Law Series, titled *Intellectual Property Law: Copyright, Patents, Trade-Marks*, David Vaver notes that "early in its history, Canada came to protect foreign authors and enterprises alongside its native born—at least its native born descended from settlers."[37] Vaver further states, "Both the Paris and Berne conventions were highly Eurocentric treaties that ignored the culture of indigenous peoples."[38] Native culture was thought to be free for the taking, the product of many and so the preserve of none—except when it was transformed by the mediation of Europeans, whereupon it magically gained cultural legitimacy. Although TK can have fundamental characteristics that differ from European-based intellectual property, Traditional Knowledge *is* intellectual property owned collectively by Indigenous Nations or groupings therein. However, this collective ownership is not acknowledged by the IPR system.

Case Studies in IPR/TK Interface

This section will detail examples of Traditional Knowledge that have been mis-appropriated and otherwise protected or unprotected under copyright, patents, and trademarks. The case studies will be analyzed in terms of the insights they provide about the functionality of the intellectual property rights system and its ability to incorporate TK and the interests of Indigenous Peoples—where TK originates. The section will highlight concerns that existing regimes of protection are not able to protect certain forms of TK; and, therefore, will support the argument that new systems of protection need to be developed and implemented (that could both include, and work in conjunction with, Indigenous Customary Law). The three main mechanisms of the IPR system—copyright, patent, and trademark—will be examined through specific cases to show how they have impacted TK. Through the examination of the case studies, some brief analysis of how each mechanism interacted with TK will also be provided.

Interaction between TK and IPR Systems

As stated earlier, in the process of transporting European institutions into various parts of the world occupied by Indigenous Peoples, the intellectual property rights system has now been imposed upon the Traditional Knowledge system. Many issues have arisen in the past ten years regarding problems resulting from the existing IPR system's apparent inability to protect TK. The main problems with TK protection in the IPR system are

> that expressions of TK often cannot qualify for protection because they are too old and are, therefore, supposedly in the public domain;
>
> that the "author" of the material is often not identifiable and there is thus no "rights holder" in the usual sense of the term;
>
> that TK is owned "collectively" by Indigenous Peoples for cultural claims and not by individuals or corporations for economic claims.

The Public Domain Problem

Under the intellectual property rights system, knowledge and creative ideas that are not "protected" are in the public domain (i.e., they are accessible by the public). Generally, Indigenous Peoples have not used IPR to protect their knowledge, and so Traditional Knowledge is often treated as if it is in the public domain without regard for Customary Laws. Another key problem for TK is that the IPR system's concept of the public domain is based on the premise that *the author/ creator deserves recognition and compensation for his/her work because it is the product of his/her genius, but that all of society must eventually be able to benefit from that genius.* Therefore, according to this aspect of IPR theory, all knowledge and creative ideas must eventually enter the public domain. Under IPR theory, this is the reasoning behind the time period limitations associated with copyright, patents, and trademarks.

The precept that all intellectual property, including Traditional Knowledge, is intended to eventually enter the public domain is a problem for Indigenous Peoples because Customary Law dictates that certain aspects of TK are not intended for external access and use in any form. Examples of this include Sacred Ceremonial Masks; songs and dances; various forms of shamanic art; Sacred Stories; prayers; songs; ceremonies; art objects with strong spiritual significance such as scrolls, petroglyphs, and decorated staffs; rattles; blankets; Medicine Bundles and clothing adornments; and various sacred symbols, designs, crests, medicines, and motifs. However, the present reality is that Traditional Knowledge is, or will be, in the public domain (i.e., the intellectual property rights system overrides Customary Law).

Case Studies

After providing some background as to the key reasons behind the IPR systems' deficiencies in protecting Traditional Knowledge, the remainder of this section turns to some specific examples. Indeed, there are hundreds of such case studies, many of which are referred to in literature and discourse. However, for the purposes of illustration, the number of case studies will be limited to two or three under the categories of copyright, patent, and trademark. The cases will attempt to show that an intellectual/legal analysis of reasons for IPR deficiencies can be made simpler by looking at some concrete examples. An effort has also been made to provide a balance between positive and negative examples in terms of IPR/TK interaction in the selection of the cases.

Copyright Cases

This section will first contrast two cases where Indigenous stories have been published in children's books. The first case is one in which a non-Indigenous author overtly appropriated and copyrighted stories. The second case involved an Indigenous publisher who attempted to adopt aspects of Customary Law into the publishing process. A third example of a case of music copyright is also included.

THE CAMERON CASE. In 1985, the Euro-Canadian author Anne Cameron began publishing a series of children's books through Harbour Publications based on West Coast Indigenous Traditional Stories. These books include *The Raven, Raven and Snipe, Keeper of the River, How the Loon Lost Her Voice, Orca's Song, Raven Returns the Water, Spider Woman, Lazy Boy,* and *Raven Goes Berrypicking.* Cameron had heard the Traditional Stories by Indigenous storytellers and/or had been present at occasions when the stories were recited. The original printing of the books granted Anne Cameron sole authorship, copyright, and royalty beneficiary, and gave no credit to the Indigenous origins of the stories. As the discourse around Indigenous cultural appropriation emerged in the 1990s, Cameron's books came under severe Indigenous criticism, not only on the grounds of cultural appropriation, but also because the Indigenous TK-holders asserted that some of the stories and aspects of the stories were incorrect. This led to a major confrontation with Indigenous women authors at the Third International Women's Book Fair in Montreal in 1988.[39] At the end of the confrontation, Cameron agreed not to publish any more Indigenous stories in the series. However, the books continued to be reprinted and new books in the series continued to be published. Some minor concessions have been made in subsequent reprints of books in the series, as well as in new additions to the series. Reprints of the books that were produced after 1993–1994 contained the disclaimer: "When I was growing up on Vancouver Island I met a woman who was a storyteller. She shared many stories with me and later gave me permission to share them with others . . . the woman's name was Klopimum." However, Cameron continued to maintain sole author credit, copyright, and royalty payments. In a further concession, the 1998 new addition to the series, *T'aal: The One Who Takes Bad Children*, is co-authored by Anne Cameron and the Indigenous Elder/ storyteller Sue Pielle, who also shares copyright and royalties.

THE KOU-SKELOWH CASE. The Kou-Skelowh Series, published by Theytus Books, could be viewed as proper and ethical process within Indigenous cultural confines. The series contains traditional Okanagan stories that have been translated into English, illustrated, and made into children's books. The original Kou-Skelowh Series was published by Theytus Books in 1984. The redesigned, second versions of the series were published by Theytus in 1991. One of the most valuable aspects of the series is how its development attempted to incorporate Indigenous cultural protocols into the publishing process. First, in the early 1980s, on behalf of Theytus, Okanagan author Jeannette Armstrong approached the Okanagan Elders Council and asked if some traditional legends could be used in the project. When the Elders gave permission for three legends to be used, Armstrong then condensed the legends and translated them into English. The English versions were then taken back to the Elders Council for examination and edited until they were approved.

The Elders Council was then asked if Theytus Books could have permission to publish the stories for the book trade. After lengthy discussions, Theytus was granted permission on the grounds that several conditions were met, including that no one individual would claim ownership of the legends or benefit from the sales. The Elders Council was also then asked to name the series: *Kou-Skelowh*, meaning "we are the people." The series does not name an author; instead, each book contains the caption, "An Okanagan Legend." The series is also copyrighted to the Okanagan Tribal Council, as the Okanagan Elders Council is not an incorporated entity. The methodology implemented in the Kou-Skelowh Series could stand as a model in which concerns about Indigenous cultural Protocols were considered. The methodology that was used in the Kou-Skelowh Series could also stand as an example of the uniqueness of Indigenous editorial practice.

THE MBUBE CASE. In its original Indigenous version, the "Mbube Song" is traditionally sung with a Zulu refrain that sounds, to English-speaking people, like "wimoweh." "Mbube" was a big hit throughout Southern Africa, selling nearly one hundred thousand copies in the 1940s of the recorded version by South African singer Solomon Linda, who was regarded as the master singer of the song. Linda recorded the tune in 1939, with his group the Evening Birds, and it was so popular that a style of Zulu choral music became known as Mbube Music. Decca Records in the United States accessed a copy of the recording in the 1950s and passed it on to the singer Pete Seeger, who was apparently enchanted by Mbube, especially the "wimoweh" refrain. Seeger then recorded it with the American folk group, the Weavers. American musicologists claim the song really gained notoriety with the Weavers' live version at Carnegie Hall in 1957. Linda was not credited as the writer; it was credited to Paul Campbell, a member of the folk group. The Kingston Trio released their version in 1959, with the writer credit listed as "traditional; adapted and arranged by Campbell-Linda."

A subsequent version by the Tokens was performed in an audition with the top RCA production team of Hugo (Peretti) and Luigi (Creatore) in 1960. Hugo and Luigi decided the song needed new lyrics. With George Weiss, they keyed in on what they saw as the song's "jungle origins" and wrote "The Lion Sleeps Tonight," including the "wimoweh" refrain that was Seeger's mistranslation of Linda's original. The Tokens recorded the quintessential pop version in May 1961 at RCA Studios. The song became a huge international hit and was given another round of popularity and financial benefit when it was featured as the theme song in the Disney movie, *The Lion King*. Linda or his heirs have not received any substantial royalties from a song that is perhaps one of the most well-known worldwide hits.[40] Prior to his recent passing, Seeger made concessions with the Linda family over this issue.

ANALYSIS. While the Kou-Skelowh case shows that publishers and editors can make moral decisions to respect TK, the Cameron case shows that the copyright system does not protect Traditional Stories from appropriation should the "author" choose to continue to maintain copyright. The Indigenous TK-holders of the original stories could find no recourse within copyright law. As such, they could only make their grievances known, and together with the Indigenous women authors, make a moral appeal to the copyright holder. This appeal was only moderately effective in that it only led to some minor concessions. Although the Kou-Skelowh case is a more optimistic model for TK within copyright, it fundamentally only represents an innovative use of the system based on the good will of the publisher to respect TK protocols. In the Mbube case, Soloman Linda also had no recourse within copyright law. According to music copyright, a person(s) who does fresh work on an existing work may, however, claim to be the author of the resulting product.[41]

Patent Cases

Misappropriation of TK through patents is the area in which the greatest number of misappropriations exists, as thousands of patents on TK have been licensed to corporations and individuals worldwide. At the seventh meeting of the WIPO IGC in November 2005, a representative from the Indian national delegation quoted a recent study in which "a random selection of 300 patents in India revealed that over 200 contained TK.[42] The extent of the problem has become a major concern for WIPO, being the body that grants international patents. The organization has conducted several major research studies on the topic in recent years, some of which refer to such cases as "erroneous patents" and propose mechanisms to revoke such patent licences. Many of these controversial patent licences pit small Indigenous communities against large national and multinational corporations. Noting that there is a wealth of test cases that could be selected, this section will examine two cases: one involving an Inuit corporation's unsuccessful attempt to patent Inuit TK in Canada, and the case of the patenting of a plant from Africa by corporations in the United States.

THE IGLOOLIK CASE. An example of the failure of the Patent Act to respond to Inuit designs is the Igloolik Floe Edge Boat Case.[43] A floe edge boat is a traditional Inuit boat used to retrieve seals shot at the floe edge (the edge of the ice floe), to set fishing nets in summer, to protect possessions on the sled when travelling by snowmobile or wet spring ice, and to store hunting or fishing equipment. In the late 1980s, the Canadian government sponsored the Eastern Arctic Scientific Research Centre to initiate a project to develop a floe edge boat that combined the traditional design with modern materials and technologies. In 1988, the Igloolik Business Association (IBA) sought to obtain a patent for the boats. The IBA thought that manufactured boats using the floe edge design would have great potential in the outdoor recreation market. To assist the IBA with its patent application, the Canadian Patents and Developments Limited (CPDL) agency initiated a preproject patent search that found patents were already held by a non-Inuit company for boats with similar structures. The CPDL letter to the IBA concluded that it was difficult for the CPDL to inventively distinguish the design from previous patents and, therefore, the IBA patent would not be granted. The option of challenging the pre-existing patent was considered by the IBA; however, it was decided that it would not likely be successful due to the high financial cost and risk involved in litigation.

THE TAUMATIN CASE. Taumatin is a natural sweetener made from the berries of the katemfe shrub that are traditionally used by Indigenous Peoples in Central

Africa. The protein is about two thousand times sweeter than sucrose without any of the health risks. In 1993, researchers from the Lucky Biotech Corporation and the University of California acquired a US patent on all transgenetic fruits, seeds, and vegetables containing the gene responsible for producing taumatin.[44] Although taumatin has still not reached the United States and other markets, with the high cost and low production scale of growing taumatin on plantations in Africa, and a $900-million-per-year, low-calorie sweetener market in the United States, it is highly likely that African katemfe plantations will not be used; as a result, the countries where katemfe is grown will not be able to benefit from exporting the berries.[45]

ANALYSIS. The Igloolik and tautmatin cases show that TK can be patented by non-Indigenous corporations, leaving the Indigenous originators with no financial benefits and no recourse other than litigation. Typically in patent challenge litigation, corporations have their own lawyers and financial resources to provide effective legal support, whereas local (Indigenous) communities rarely have such resources or advocates. Even if a case goes to court, the company may well succeed in convincing the court that its product, use, or process is sufficiently different from the original to constitute an invention.[46]

Trademark Cases

As most Indigenous communities are far behind in terms of establishing businesses, most trademarking of TK involves a non-Indigenous corporation trademarking an Indigenous symbol, design, or name. This practice has been curtailed by laws in the Philippines, the United States, and other countries. However, it remains rampant in most countries around the globe (for instance, the 2010 Vancouver Olympics logo). Again, many cases could have been examined in this chapter, but only two have been chosen: one case involving the Snumeymux Band trademarking petroglyphs through the Canadian Patent Office, and one involving an international corporation's patent licence being the subject of an intense international Indigenous lobbying effort.

THE SNUMEYMUX CASE. The Snumeymux people have several ancient petroglyphs located off their reserve lands near False Narrows on Gabriola Island, British Columbia. In the early 1990s, non-Indigenous residents of Gabriola Island began using some of the petroglyph images in coffee shops and various other business logos. In the mid-1990s, the Island's music festival named itself after what had become the local name of the most well-known petroglyph image: the dancing man. The Dancing Man Music Festival then adopted the image of the dancing man as the festival logo and used it on brochures, posters, advertisements, and T-shirts. The Snumeymux Band first made unsuccessful appeals to the festival, businesses, and the Gabriola Island community to stop using the petroglyph symbols. In 1998, the Snumeymux Band hired Murray Brown as its legal counsel to seek protection of the petroglyphs. At a 1998 meeting with Brown, Snumeymux Elders, and community members, the Dancing Man Festival and Gabriola Island business and community representatives were still defiant that they had a right to use the images from the petroglyphs.[47]

On the advice of Brown, the Snumeymux Band filed for a Section 91(n) Public Authority Trademark for eight petroglyphs and was awarded the trademark in October of 1998.[48] The trademark protects the petroglyphs from "all uses" by non-Snumeymux people and, therefore, the Dancing Man Festival and Gabriola Island business and community representatives were forced to stop using images derived from the petroglyphs.

THE AVEDA CASE. In 2000, the Aveda Corporation, headquartered in Minneapolis and New York City, introduced a cosmetic product line called "Indigenous," which included an aroma candle, essential oil, and hair and body shampoo. The products in the line were infused with cedar, sage, and sweetgrass, and the symbol of the line featured on all labelling and promotional material was the Medicine Wheel. The trademark application, No. 75/76,418 under the word "Indigenous," was filed with the United States Patent and Trademark Office on September 9, 1999, and was granted on November 15, 1999. The "Indigenous" trademark application was submitted to the Canadian Intellectual Property Office on September 15, 1999, and granted on July 16, 2003.

Indigenous lobbying against the "Indigenous" line began to grow throughout 2000–2002 in the United States, Australia, and New Zealand. The lobbying efforts attempted to disseminate the message that the line was offensive to Indigenous Peoples, mainly because the word "Indigenous" was trademarked by a non-Indigenous corporation, and the Medicine Wheel symbol was being used in a culturally inappropriate manner. The cross-cultural issues were somewhat clouded by the fact that the cedar, sage, and sweetgrass were obtained from Native Americans and other Native Americans endorsed the products. For instance, Robby Romero, president of Native Children's Survival, made the following statement that was printed on one of the brochures: "Indigenous™ express[es] a reverence to Mother Earth, devotion to the environment, and an alliance with Wisdom Keepers of the World."

Eventually, Indigenous lobbyists from the United States and Australia began working together and managed to arrange a meeting with Dominique Conseil, Aveda's president, in September 2003. In the meeting, Conseil was persuaded to drop the line and the trademark, and Aveda issued the following statement in a press release dated November 4, 2003:

> *Aveda Corporation today announced the discontinuation of its Indigenous product line as well as its intention to abandon the "Indigenous" trademark. The Indigenous collection ... will cease production immediately.... The decision was reached following a meeting among representatives of several*

indigenous nations of the Americas and Australia and representatives of Aveda. . . . We are discontinuing the Indigenous product line to demonstrate our ongoing support and respect for indigenous peoples in their efforts to protect their traditional knowledge and resources . . . Aveda will discontinue marketing any products under the "Indigenous" trademark and, to emphasize its respect, will begin the formalities necessary to abandon any rights it may have in this trademark . . . By its action, Aveda also hopes to stand in solidarity with indigenous peoples in their quest for recognition of intellectual property rights in their traditional wisdom.[49]

ANALYSIS. While the outcomes of the Snumeymux and Aveda cases appear to shed an optimistic light on trademark protection of TK, a closer examination of the cases still reveals problems with TK and IPR interaction. The Snumeymux trademark did "work" to protect the petroglyphs but not as the trademark system is intended. According to trademark theory, the system is intended to be "offensive," allowing the rights holder to freely use the mark for the promotion and advancement of the product into the marketplace. In the Snumeymux case, the petroglyphs were trademarked for "defensive" purposes—that is, so they would not be used. Like the Kou-Skelowh case, the Snumeymux case represents an innovative use of the IPR system that negotiated within the system's limitations and found a way to make it work to protect TK.

The Aveda case may be a great Indigenous lobbying victory, but it is not such a great victory for TK protection within the IPR system. In this case, the extenuating circumstances of a strong and organized lobby, a company eager to protect its naturalist, purest, earthy image, and an open-minded company president, led to the cancelling of the line and the trademark. However, like the author Anne Cameron's minor concessions, the cancelling was the result of a willing concession on the part of the rights holder based on a moral appeal. There is nothing within the IPR system that would have compelled Aveda to abandon the mark if the company, for example, chose to make an economic decision based on investment in developing and manufacturing the line, and ignore the moral issue presented before it.

Summary of Case Studies

The case studies have shown that serious conflicts exist between the IPR and TK systems that leads to the conclusion that it constitutes a major problem that Indigenous Peoples must resolve with the modern states they are within and with the international community. In contrast to Eurocentric thought, almost all Indigenous thought asserts that property is a sacred, ecological order and manifestations of that order should not be treated as commodities.[50] It is clear that there are pressing problems in the regulation of TK. It is also clear that the IPR system and other Eurocentric concepts do not offer a solution to some of the problems. There have been cases of Indigenous Peoples using the IPR system to protect their TK. However, the reality is that there are many more cases of non-Indigenous people using the IPR system to take ownership over TK by using copyright, trademark, and especially patents. In some such cases, this has created a ridiculous situation whereby Indigenous Peoples cannot legally access their own knowledge.

A study undertaken on behalf of the Intellectual Property Policy Directorate (IPPD) of Industry Canada and the Canadian Working Group on the Convention on Biodiversity Article 8(j) concludes:

> There is little in the cases found to suggest that the Intellectual Property system has adapted very much to the unique aspects of Indigenous knowledge or heritage. Rather, Indigenous peoples have been required to conform to the legislation that was designed for other contexts and purposes, namely western practices and circumstances. At the same time, there is little evidence that these changes have been promoted within the system, i.e., from failed efforts to use it that have been challenged (IPPD-2002).

Such conclusions, among many being drawn in other countries and international forums, and the case study examples discussed here, support the argument that new systems of protection need to be developed. *Sui Generis* models based on and/or incorporating customary laws have been proposed and developed in many countries and are being discussed in the WIPO IGC.

Terra Nullius and the Colonization of Traditional Knowledge

Between thirty thousand and 520 years ago, Traditional Knowledge systems developed and thrived, protected and regulated by their associated Customary Laws, upon approximately 90 per cent of the earth's landmass that was occupied by thousands of Indigenous Nations. In this pre-colonization era, Indigenous Peoples were most of the world population and lived in balance with natural laws in their respective Territories. In the early colonial period, Western perspectives interpreted Indigenous Nations through the lens of Social Darwinism as subhuman and primitive. Consequently, despite its immense universal value, TK was also seen by the Western perspective to be of little or no value. Christopher Columbus came to Indigenous America as an invader and a colonizer without regard for the original inhabitants he "discovered."[51] The arrival of Columbus signified the beginning of a period of colonization in which Indigenous Peoples were subjected to Western legal norms in replacement of their own. By 1493, the patterns were set for the next 520 years in the Americas and other places where European colonizers relocated and dispossessed Indigenous Peoples from their Territories and resources.[52] Throughout the early period of colonization, debates and discussions around Europe considered whether Indigenous Peoples were human beings or not, largely concluding the latter. Theories of Social Darwinism added further justification that Indigenous, black, and other brown-skinned peoples were lesser evolved than Western European peoples.

Indigenous Peoples' Territories were interpreted by Western legal regimes as being *terra nullius*, literally meaning "land belonging to no one." *Terra nullius* justified the idea and legal concept that when the first Europeans arrived, the land was owned by no one and therefore open to settlement. In the sixteenth century, when Spanish, British, and French colonial forces began large-scale encroachment upon the thirty million Indigenous people in North America, *terra nullius*, Social Darwinism, and the Doctrine of Discovery were the dominant ideologies that prevailed through colonial institutions to many current, modern, Western institutions.

North American Colonization and Residential Schools

Early settlers in North America benefitted from Indigenous Peoples sharing their Traditional Environmental Knowledge, especially in the Arctic and semi-Arctic regions of the continent—now Canada. This early history of the relationship between the British Crown/Canada and Indigenous Nations was based on international law, nation-to-nation negotiations, and treaties. However, soon afterward, Canada began to stray down a path leading away from international law toward an adversarial/hostile, dominating relationship with Indigenous Peoples. This era continues through to today, including the residential school system and several other breaches of international law. With the Act for the Gradual Civilization of Indian Tribes of 1851, Upper and Lower Canada began passing laws designed to eliminate Indigenous Peoples without their consent. In this era, the government viewed Indigenous Peoples as an obstacle to acquiring complete control of the resources and territories of Canada. It began to speak of "the Indian Problem." With the implementation of an official policy of assimilation carried out through the Indian Act of 1876, the colonial project was in full force.

Throughout the period of 1879 to the late 1980s, the Canadian government, in conjunction with Catholic, Protestant, and Anglican churches, displaced whole generations of Indigenous children from their homes, families, Elders, and communities into the Indian residential school (IRS) system. The vision was anchored in the fundamental belief that to educate Indigenous children effectively, they had to be separated from their families, thereby suggesting that the parenting process in Indigenous communities had to be disrupted.[53] The children were taught to be ashamed of who they were, and they were physically, mentally, and sexually abused. Thousands lost their lives at these schools, many due to disease.[54] The IRS system was the hallmark institution of the assimilation policy. In 1920, Canadian Superintendent of Indian Affairs Duncan Campbell Scott made his (in)famous statement, "Our object is to continue until there is not a single Indian in Canada that has not been absorbed into the body politic."[55]

The overriding goal of the IRS system was to divest Indigenous Peoples of their TK, and thereby their attachment to (and knowledge related to) their Territories forevermore within a few generations. In the schools, children were punished for displaying all aspects of their original cultures. Resetting the child's cultural clock from the "savage" setting—the seasonal round of hunting and gathering—to the hourly and daily precision required by an industrial order was seen by the Department of Indian Affairs as an issue of primary consideration.[56] As Indigenous Peoples were being divested of their TK throughout the IRS era, some of the following disciplines and third parties were actively engaging in the following practices: 1) anthropologists, archaeologists, and some missionary groups were in the process of documenting TK in data banks; 2) museums and collectors were confiscating Indigenous cultural materials containing and representing TK; 3) third-party corporations were appropriating Indigenous artistic designs, such as symbols and totem poles, and functional designs, such as canoes and snowshoes; and 4) Canada was developing its IPR regime while at the same time subjecting TK and Indigenous Peoples to it. This was the era of intense colonization and was the first wide-scale colonization of TK. The impacts of residential schools are not buried in the past; they continue through the ongoing loss of TK and other multigenerational traumatic effects. Still many Canadians today are unaware of the impacts of residential schools, including the loss and colonization of TK.

Gnaritas Nullius (No One's Knowledge)

Just as Indigenous territories were declared *terra nullius* in the colonization process, so, too, has TK been treated as *gnaritas nullius* (no one's knowledge) by the IPR system, which has meant it has consequently flowed into the public domain along with Western knowledge. In effect, Indigenous knowledge has been colonized, along with many other Indigenous institutions and possessions. In this colonization process based on *gnaritas nullius*, manifestations of, and practices derived from, Indigenous knowledge—such as the canoe and kayak design, bungee jumping, snowshoes, lacrosse, surfing, and sustainable development—are embraced by Western peoples as their own (without acknowledgement of the source), just as lands were taken in the colonization process based on *terra nullius*. This has occurred despite widespread Indigenous claims of ownership and breach of Customary Law. The problem is that advocates for the public domain seem to see knowledge as the same concept across cultures, and impose the liberal ideals of freedom and equality to Indigenous knowledge systems. Not all knowledge has the same role and significance within diverse epistemologies, nor do diverse world views all necessarily incorporate a principle that knowledge can be universally accessed. Neither can all knowledge fit into Western paradigms and legal regimes.

A central dimension of Indigenous knowledge systems is that knowledge is shared according to developed rules and expectations for behaviour within frameworks that have been developed and practised over millennia. Arguments for a public domain of Indigenous knowledge again reduce the capacity for Indigenous People's control and decision making over their knowledge and cannot be reasonably made outside the problematic frameworks of the colonization of TK and *gnaritas nullius*. Intellectual property law is largely European in derivation and promotes particular cultural interpretations of knowledge, ownership, authorship, private property, and monopoly privilege. Indigenous Peoples do not necessarily interpret or conceptualize their knowledge systems and knowledge practices in the same way or only through these concepts.[57] Thus, Indigenous Peoples and their allies continue to argue for recognition of the jurisdiction of Customary Law over Indigenous knowledge and the development of *sui generis* regimes that incorporate and complement Customary Laws at local, national, and international United Nations levels such as the WIPO IGC.

NOTES

1   Catherine Hoppers, ed., *Indigenous Knowledge and the Integration of Knowledge Systems: Towards a Philosophy of Articulation* (Claremont, South Africa: New Africa Books, 2002), 11.

2   Jack Weatherford, *Indian Givers: How Native Americans Transformed the World* (New York: Crown Publishers, 1988), 59.

3   Daniel Francis, *The Imaginary Indian: The Image of the Indian in Canadian Culture* (Vancouver: Arsenal Pulp Press, 1992), 193.

4   Peter Nabokov and Robert O. B. Easton, *Native American Architecture* (Oxford: Oxford University Press, 1989), 12.

5   Weatherford, *Indian Givers*, 85.

6   Lee Francis, *Native Time: A Historical Time Line of Native America* (New York: St. Martin's Griffin, 1996), 14.

7   Ibid.

8   Sakej Henderson, "Traditional Indigenous Knowledge" (unpublished manuscript, 2004), 1.

9   Ibid., 6.

10 Sakej Henderson, "Postcolonial Indigenous Legal Consciousness," *Indigenous Law Journal* 1 (Spring 2002): 1–56.

11 Ibid., 2.

12 World Intellectual Property Organization (WIPO), International Committee on Intellectual Property and Genetic Resources, Traditional Knowledge, and Folklore, *Traditional Knowledge: Operational Terms and Definitions*. Third Session (Geneva, Switzerland: WIPO, June 13–21, 2002).

13 Vine Deloria Jr., *Red Earth, White Lies: Native Americans and the Myth of Scientific Fact* (New York: Scribner, 1995), 42.

14 Vivien Burr, *An Introduction to Social Constructionism* (New York: Routledge, 1995).

15 Kenneth J. Gergen, "The Social Constructionist Movement in Modern Psychology," *American Psychologist* 40, no. 3 (March 1985): 266–275, http://dx.doi.org/10.1037/0003-066X.40.3.266.

16 Wikipedia, "Epistemology," http://en.wikipedia.org/wiki/Epistemology.

17 Louise J. Phillips and Marianne W. Jorgensen, *Discourse Analysis as Theory and Method* (London: Sage Publications, 2002), 5.

18 Ibid., 5.

19 Jo-ann Archibald, *Indigenous Storywork: Educating the Heart, Mind, Body and Spirit* (Vancouver: University of British Columbia Press, 2008), 63.

20 Charles Royal, "An Organic Arising: An Interpretation of Tikanga Based upon Maori Creation Traditions" (unpublished manuscript, 2007).

21 Linda Tuhiwai Smith, *Decolonizing Methodologies: Research and Indigenous Peoples* (London: Zed Books, 1999), 147.

22 Shirley Sterling, "The Grandmother Stories: Oral Tradition and the Transmission of Culture" (PhD dissertation, University of British Columbia, 1997), 39.

23 Merle Alexander, "Customary Laws: Appling Sharing within Communities to International Instruments" (unpublished manuscript, 2003), 9.

24 See John Borrows, *Canada's Indigenous Constitution* (Toronto: University of Toronto Press, 2010); Hoppers, *Indigenous Knowledge and the Integration of Knowledge Systems*, 17–20, for an interpretation of an Anishinabek resource law regarding Nanabush v. Deer, Wolf et al.

25 Alexander, "Customary Laws," 11.

26 Henderson, "Traditional Indigenous Knowledge," 9.

27 Susan Crean, Caldwell Taylor, and Gregory Younging, *Handbook on Creator's Rights* (Toronto: Creator's Rights Alliance, 2003).

28 Ibid., 8.

29 Ibid.,10.

30 Ibid., 16.

31 Universal Declaration of Human Rights, December 10, 1948, UN General Assembly Res. 217.

32 Berne Convention for the Protection of Literary and Artistic Works, September 9, 1886, as revised at Paris on July 24, 1971, and amended in 1979, S. Treaty Doc. No. 99–27 (1986).

33 Ibid.

34 Ibid.

35 David Vaver, *Intellectual Property Law: Copyright, Patents, Trade-Marks* (Concord, ON: Irwin Law, 1997), 1.

36 Ibid., 120.

37 Ibid.

38 Ibid., 2.

39 Laura Smyth Groening, *Listening to Old Woman Speak: Natives and alterNatives in Canadian Literature* (Montreal: McGill University Press, 2004).

40 Bill Brent and Fred Glenman, "Translated Hits," http://www.bobshanon.com/stories/hesofine.htmlQ2.

41 Vaver, *Intellectual Property Law*.

42 WIPO Intergovernmental Committee on Intellectual Property and Genetic Resources, Traditional Knowledge and Folklore: Seventh Session (WIPO/GRTKF/IC/7), intervention of Indian delegation, http://www.wipo.int/meetings/en/details.jsp?meeting_id=6183.

43 Violet Ford, "The Protection of Inuit Cultural Property" (paper presented at the meeting of the Creator's Rights Alliance National Conference on Traditional Knowledge, Montreal, QC, June 4, 2004), 20.

44 Gregory Younging, "Competing Jurisdictions over Traditional Knowledge in the North Americas," (presentation to the WIPO Panel on Indigenous and Local Communities' Concerns and Experiences in Promoting, Sustaining and Safeguarding Their Traditional Knowledge, Traditional Cultural Expressions and Genetic Resources, Intergovernmental Committee on Intellectual Property and Genetic Resources, Traditional Knowledge and Folklore, Tenth Session, Geneva, Switzerland, November 30, 2006).

45 Darrell Posey and Graham Duttleid, *Beyond Intellectual Property: Toward Traditional Resource Rights for Indigenous Peoples and Local Communities* (Ottawa, ON: International Development Research Centre, 1996), 82.

46 Ibid., 94.

47 Michael Brown, *Who Owns Native Culture?* (Cambridge, MA: First Harvard University Press, 2003).

48 Ibid.

49 "Aveda Announces Discontinuation of Indigenous Product Collection," media release, November 11, 2003, http://ip.aaas.org/tekindex.nsf/9703c8d7edc467d685256ae10074187f/e632f81fb2b671b085256ddc00545a9e?OpenDocumentQ3.

50 Marie Battiste and James Youngblood Henderson, *Protecting Indigenous Knowledge and Heritage: A Global Challenge* (Saskatoon, SK: Purich Publishing, 2001), 145.

51 Sharron Venne, *Our Elders Understand Our Rights: Evolving International Law Regarding Indigenous Rights* (Penticton, BC: Theytus Books, 1998), 2.

52 Ibid., 4.

53 John Milloy, *A National Crime: The Canadian Government and the Residential School System* (Winnipeg, MB: University of Manitoba Press, 1999), 23.

54 Connie Walker, "New Documents May Shed Light on Residential School Deaths," CBC, January 7, 2014, http://www.cbc.ca/news/aboriginal/new-documents-may-shed-light-on-residential-school-deaths-1.2487015.

55 Duncan Campbell Scott, cited in John Leslie, *The Historical Development of the Indian Act*, second edition (Ottawa: Department of Indian Affairs and Northern Development, Treaties and Historical Research Branch, 1978), 114.

56 Ibid., 36.

57 Jane Anderson, "Indigenous/Traditional Knowledge & Intellectual Property," Center for the Study of the Public Domain, Duke University School of Law, 2010, http://www.law.duke.edu/cspd/itkpaper.

NOTES

1. Atwood, *Survival*, 91.
2. Mihesuah, *So You Want to Write About American Indians*, 9.
3. Mihesuah, 24.
4. The draft principles produced through this program in 2015 by the Indigenous Editors Circle are included as an appendix in this guide.
5. Jenness, *The Indians of Canada*, 1.
6. Berkhofer, *The White Man's Indian*, 27.
7. Adams, *A Tortured People*, 33.
8. See the essay "Gnaritas Nullius (No One's Knowledge): the Essence of Traditional Knowledge and Its Colonization through Western Legal Regimes," which is an appendix in this guide. This essay provides a detailed understanding of what Traditional Knowledge is and how it often conflicts with intellectual property rights law. The essay also includes the WIPO definition of Traditional Knowledge, which is widely considered the standard definition. Article 31 of the United Nations Declaration on the Rights of Indigenous Peoples also provides good insights into Traditional Knowledge and Indigenous Peoples' jurisdiction over it.
9. Blaeser, *Akwe:kon Journal*, 35–41.
10. Lutz, *Contemporary Challenges*, 31.
11. Unless otherwise specified, this work follows the *Guide to Acknowledging First Peoples & Traditional Territory* (September 2017) by the Canadian Association of University Teachers (CAUT) for the names of Indigenous Peoples and their spellings. The CAUT guide complies these names and spellings in consultation with Indigenous Peoples.
12. United Nations General Assembly, Declaration on the Rights of Indigenous Peoples, 11–12.
13. "Fully adopting UNDRIP," *Northern Public Affairs*, 11 May 2016.
14. Australia Council for the Arts, *Protocols for Producing Indigenous Australian Writing*, 9.
15. Australia Council for the Arts, 8.
16. Australia Council for the Arts, 4.
17. Younging, "Protocols Provide Guidelines for Behaviour," 11.

18. Archibald, *Indigenous Storywork*, 13.
19. Australia Council for the Arts, 17.
20. Australia Council for the Arts, 16.
21. Vowel, *Indigenous Writes*, 8.
22. Vowel, 7.
23. Royal Commission on Aboriginal Peoples, *Report of the Royal Commission on Aboriginal Peoples, Volume 2: Restructuring the Relationship,* 246.
24. Truth and Reconciliation Commission of Canada, *Calls to Action,* 5.
25. Mohawk, "Indian History through Indian Eyes," 104.
26. The names and spellings in this list follow the *Guide to Acknowledging First Peoples & Traditional Territory* (September 2017) by the Canadian Association of University Teachers (CAUT), and the *First Nations Names Authority List* developed by the X̱wi7x̱wa Library, University of British Columbia. Consult the appendix in this guide on these resources for more information.
27. Alcantara, Lalonde, and Wilson, "Indigenous Research and Academic Freedom," 1–2.
28. Vowel, 9.
29. Weaver, *That the People Might Live,* 9.
30. Weaver, 89.
31. Armstrong, *Slash,* 15.
32. Campbell, *Stories of the Road Allowance People,* 19.
33. Cuddon, *The Penguin Dictionary of Literary Terms and Literary Theory,* 659.
34. Marken, foreword to *Stories of the Road Allowance People,* 5.
35. Lowes, *Indian Giver,* 19.
36. Andra-Warner, *The Mounties,* 47; Dempsey, *Crowfoot,* 78; MacEwan, *Coyote Music,* 26.

BIBLIOGRAPHY

"Fully Adopting UNDRIP: Minister Bennett's Speech at the United Nations." *Northern Public Affairs*, 11 May 2016. http://www.northernpublicaffairs.ca/index/fully-adopting-undrip-minister-bennetts-speech/

Adams, Howard. *A Tortured People: The Politics of Colonization*. Penticton, BC: Theytus Books, 1995.

Alcantara, Christopher, Dianne Lalonde, and Gary N. Wilson. "Indigenous Research and Academic Freedom: A View from Political Scientists." *The International Indigenous Policy Journal* 8, no. 2 (2017): 1–19.

Andra-Warner, Elle. *The Mounties: Tales of Adventure and Danger from the Early Days*. Surrey, BC: Heritage House Publishing, 2009.

Archibald, Jo-ann. *Indigenous Storywork: Educating the Heart, Mind, Body, and Spirit*. Vancouver: UBC Press, 2008.

Armstrong, Jeannette. *Slash*. Penticton, BC: Theytus Books, 1985.

Atwood, Margaret. *Survival: A Thematic Guide to Canadian Literature*. Toronto: House of Anansi, 1972.

Australia Council for the Arts. *Protocols for Producing Indigenous Australian Writing*. Strawberry Hills, Australia: Arts Council, 2007. http://www.australiacouncil.gov.au/symphony/extension/richtext_redactor/getfile/?name=fc8a5cc73467cb405e8943ae14975da7.pdf

Berkhofer, Robert, Jr. *The White Man's Indian: Images of the American Indian from Columbus to the Present*. New York: Vintage, 1979.

Blaeser, Kim. "Returning the Gift: North American Native Writers' Festival." *Akwe:kon Journal* 10, no. 1 (Spring 1993): 35–41.

Campbell, Maria. *Stories of the Road Allowance People*. Penticton, BC: Theytus Books, 1995.

Canadian Association of University Teachers. *Guide to Acknowledging First Peoples & Traditional Territories*. Ottawa: CAUT, September 2017. https://www.caut.ca/sites/default/files/caut-guide-to-acknowledging-first-peoples-and-traditional-territory-2017-09.pdf

Cuddon, J. A. *The Penguin Dictionary of Literary Terms and Literary Theory*. 3rd ed. Toronto: Penguin Canada, 1992.

Dempsey, Hugh A. *Crowfoot*. Halifax: Formac Publishing, 2015.

Jenness, Diamond. *The Indians of Canada*. 6th ed. Toronto: University of Toronto Press, 1963.

Lowes, Warren. *Indian Giver: A Legacy of North American Native Peoples*. Penticton, BC: Theytus Books, 1986.

Lutz, Hartmut. *Contemporary Challenges: Conversations with Canadian Native Authors*. Saskatoon, SK: Fifth House Publishers, 1991.

MacEwan, Grant. *Coyote Music and Other Humorous Tales of the Early West*. Calgary: Rocky Mountain Books, 1993.

Marken, Ron. *Foreword to Stories of the Road Allowance People, by Maria Campbell*. Penticton, BC: Theytus Books, 1995.

Mihesuah, Devon Abbott. *So You Want to Write About American Indians: A Guide for Writers, Students, and Scholars*. Lincoln: University of Nebraska Press, 2005.

Mohawk, John. "Indian History through Indian Eyes." In *Gatherings: The Enowkin Journal of First North American People, Volume II, Two Faces: Unmasking the Facts of our Divided Nations*, edited by Florene Belmore and Greg Younging, 17–32. Penticton, BC: Theytus Books, 1991.

Royal Commission on Aboriginal Peoples. *Restructuring the Relationship*. vol. 2. Report of the Royal Commission on Aboriginal Peoples. Ottawa: Canada Communication Group Publishing, 1996.

Truth and Reconciliation Commission of Canada. *Truth and Reconciliation Commission of Canada: Calls to Action*. Winnipeg: Truth and Reconciliation Commission of Canada, 2015.

United Nations General Assembly. Resolution 61/295. United Nations Declaration on the Rights of Indigenous Peoples. March 2008. http://www.un.org/esa/socdev/unpfii/documents/DRIPS_en.pdf

Vowel, Chelsea. *Indigenous Writes: A Guide to First Nations, Métis and Inuit Issues in Canada*. Winnipeg: Highwater Press, 2016.

Weaver, Jace. *That the People Might Live: Native American Literatures and Native American Community*. New York: Oxford University Press, 1997.

Xwi7xwa Library. *First Nations Names Authority List*. Vancouver: University of British Columbia, March 2009. http://xwi7xwa.library.ubc.ca/files/2011/09/bcfn.pdf

Younging, Gregory. "Protocols Provide Guidelines for Behaviour." In the Proceedings of the Cultural Protocols & the Arts Forum, Penticton, BC, March 2014. http://www.fpcc.ca/files/PDF/Arts/FPCC_Cultural__Protocols_and_the_Arts_Forum_2015.pdf

INDEX

ABOUT THE AUTHOR

Gregory Younging, Opaskwayak Cree Nation, had an MA from the Institute of Canadian Studies at Carleton University, an MPub from the Canadian Centre for Studies in Writing and Publishing at Simon Fraser University, and a PhD in educational studies from the University of British Columbia. From 1990 to 2004, he was managing editor of Theytus Books, and was its publisher from 2016 to 2019. Gregory worked with both the Assembly of First Nations and the Royal Commission on Aboriginal Peoples, and was a member of the Canada Council Aboriginal Peoples Committee on the Arts from June 1997 to June 2001, and the British Columbia Arts Council from July 1999 to July 2001. He was assistant director of research for the Truth and Reconciliation Commission of Canada. He was on the faculty of the Indigenous Editors Circle at Humber College, Toronto, until 2017, and was the program coordinator for Indigenous Studies at the University of British Columbia, Okanagan, when he passed away in 2019.